GCSE BITESIZE revision

Spanish

Niobe O'Connor

Ron Wallace (GCSE examiner)

BBC

Published by BBC Educational Publishing, BBC White City,
201 Wood Lane, London W12 7TS
First published 1999, Reprinted 2000, Reprinted 2001
© Niobe O'Connor/BBC Worldwide (Educational Publishing) 1999
(Educational Publishing), 2000

ISBN: 0 563 46411 9

Designed by Ennismore Design.
Printed in Great Britain by Bell & Bain Ltd., Glasgow

📺 These instructions might well appear in your exam, so see if you can try and learn them!

Adapta ... la carta/la postal.
   Adapt ... the letter/the postcard.

Ahora mira ... los dibujos.
   Now look at ... the pictures.

Apunta ... la letra correcta/el número correcto.
   Note down ... the correct letter/number.

Busca ... el dibujo correcto.
   Look for ... the correct picture.

Busca en el texto ...   Look for ... in the text.

¿Cada frase es verdad o mentira?
   Is each sentence true or false?

Coloca las frases en el orden correcto.
   Put the sentences in the correct order.

Completa la frase siguiente.
   Complete the following sentence.

Completa ... las frases/el cuadro.
   Complete ... the sentences/the box.

Con las palabras más apropiadas.
   With the most appropriate words.

Contesta a las preguntas.
   Answer the questions.

Copia las frases que indican ...
   Copy the sentences which indicate ...

Elige/escoge la frase correcta.
   Choose the correct sentence.

Empareja las dos partes de las frases.
   Match up the sentence halves.

Empareja cada foto con la frase correcta.
   Match each photo to the correct phrase.

En la casilla más apropiada/adecuada.
   In the most appropriate box.

Escribe ✓ al lado de las frases verdaderas.
   Put a ✓ beside the true sentences.

Escribe el número en la casilla.
   Write the number in the box.

Escribe en frases en español.
   Write in sentences in Spanish.

Escribe sobre ...   Write about ...

Escribe una carta/una postal.
   Write a letter/a postcard.

Escribe tus respuestas a las preguntas.
   Write your answers to the questions.

Escribe una letra en cada casilla.
   Write a letter in each box.

Escucha a ...
   Listen to ...

Estás oyendo la radio.
   You're listening to the radio.

Escucha la conversación.
   Listen to the conversation.

Escucha los reportajes.
   Listen to the reports.

Las frases están desordenadas.
   The sentences are in the wrong order.

Lee con atención este artículo.
   Read this article carefully.

Lee este anuncio.   Read this advertisement.

Lee este trozo de un artículo.
   Read this section of an article.

Lee las 4 afirmaciones.
   Read the 4 statements.

Lee las preguntas 1–6.
   Read the questions 1–6.

Menciona 2 detalles cada vez.
   Mention 2 details each time.

Pon una señal (✓) ...   Put a (✓) ...

Pon una cruz (✗) ... Put a cross (✗) ...

Sobran 2 frases.
   There are 2 sentences left over.

Tienes que dar 6 detalles en total.
   You have to give 6 details altogether.

Vas a oír una serie de diálogos.
   You'll hear a series of dialogues.

Contents

About BITESIZEspanish

BITESIZEspanish is a revision guide that has been specially put together to help you with your GCSE exams. You can watch the TV programmes, work your way through the activities and suggestions in this book and if you feel you need more help on a specific point, you can go on-line to the website service whenever you choose, and ask the internet team to help you.

It's called BITESIZEspanish because that's a good way to do your revision – in bitesize pieces, and not in one great chunk a few days before your exam! If you have recorded the TV programmes on video, you can watch them in sections as often as you like. The book is divided into small sections that you can go through one at a time, at a pace which suits you.

About this book

The InfoZONE on page 3 gives you a list of key Spanish instructions and their English equivalents. Ask your teacher if he or she can give you a list of the instructions which your exam board uses and make sure you learn them.

Each of the sections in this book follows the same pattern, starting with an introduction and a vocabulary page. Ask your friends and family to test you on this or record the phrases on tape to learn: say the English, then leave a short gap before recording the Spanish. Try and get into the habit of listening to the tape whenever you've got a spare moment. Aim to say the Spanish aloud in the gap before you hear the answer on tape.

Next, you'll find listening activities based on the TV programmes, so make sure you video them. You can listen to them straight through or you can pause and rewind to break the programmes down into more manageable sections. Listen as often as you want to as you're not being tested here!

Speaking activities come next and you can do these on your own or work with a friend. If you find speaking in Spanish hard, try recording yourself on tape and listening to it afterwards – this will help you learn the language and get used to the sound of your own voice.

Reading activities are next, but you don't have to do them all at once. Just tackle them at your own pace. If you don't write the answers in the book, come back to a section a few weeks later and set yourself a time limit of five minutes on each activity. This will help you get up to speed for the exam.

Writing activities complete each section, but you can do them at any point. Try doing them with a friend sometimes so that you can read each other's work and give some helpful criticism – you could spot spelling mistakes, check endings on adjectives and verbs and offer helpful advice. Just seeing someone else's attempts can give you fresh ideas of your own.

Each section is full of tips to help you as you work towards the exam, but feel free to jot down your own notes in the space left in the margins.

KEY TO SYMBOLS

📺 A link to the video

(?) Something to think about

◎ An activity to do

ⓗ A higher activity – ask your teacher if you need to do these.

Getting organised

When are your Spanish GCSE exams? Remember you probably have a Speaking, Listening, Reading and Writing exam to think about. The Speaking part will almost certainly be the first and come rather earlier than the others – possibly before Easter. Make sure you have the dates written down in large writing somewhere very visible in your bedroom – it's easy to think you've got more time to revise than you actually have!

Check with your teacher what you have to do for each part of the exam, especially the Speaking part. Do you have to do a presentation? How many role-plays? How long is the conversation part? Find out if you're allowed a dictionary during the preparation time, how long this is, and whether you can take any notes you make during that time into the exam with you.

Make sure you know exactly which sections of the exam you're doing: there are usually Foundation and Higher papers and you might be able to choose a combination which plays to your particular strengths. Some boards allow you to make a decision on the day of the Speaking exam itself as to whether you do the Higher part or not – does yours?

Count the number of days left before the exam and decide how you're going to allocate your revision time. There are five sections to BITESIZEspanish: three of them have 16 pages and two have 18. How many pages will you tackle a week? Break it down next into days, then hours and minutes. Don't make your revision sessions too long – it's often better to do a small amount every day rather than a larger chunk once a week. Draw up an action plan for yourself and try to stick to it.

Once you've made your plan, you can start revising. Make sure that:

- you've got a quiet place to work
- you've got all you need: video, book, pencil, dictionary, internet access …
- you don't allow yourself to be distracted by the TV, radio, magazines …
- you keep the revision session short and focused so you avoid getting tired or demotivated.

On the day

Here are a few helpful hints for the day(s) of the exam(s):

- Make sure you know when your exam is (morning or afternoon) and where it is.
- Arrive in plenty of time, with everything you need: several pens, a pencil, a ruler and a dictionary.
- Don't try to do any last minute revising on your way to the exam – just concentrate on saying a few things to yourself in Spanish, like the numbers, the days of the week or the months of the year. If you've got time, listen to a Spanish tape to get yourself into a Spanish 'mood'.

Good luck with your revision – and good luck in your exam.
¡Buena suerte a todos!

THE ON-LINE SERVICE
You can find extra support, activities, tips and answers to your exam queries on the BITESIZE website. The address is http://www.bbc.co.uk/education/revision

Everyday Activities

This section is about

- School

- Life at home

- Health and fitness

- Food and drink

This section is all about everyday activities, and that includes school, life at home, feeling ill, staying healthy and eating at home or in a restaurant. In the exam, you'll be expected to be able to talk and write about these topics. You'll have to ask and answer questions about them, give details and descriptions and understand what life is like in Spanish-speaking countries. This section will help you with all of this, so read on!

School

Let's start with school (el instituto/el colegio). Schools in Spain often start earlier than in Britain – some as early as eight o'clock – and many finish around two o'clock. Spanish pupils have most of their lessons in one classroom, so the teachers move around between lessons. In many schools pupils call their teacher by his or her first name – but still using the polite form of address (usted). In some areas, there are two sessions of school: the usual one in the morning for younger pupils and a later one from four till nine for older pupils (nocturno).

Life at home

In town centres, many people live in flats (pisos/apartamentos). These often have a balcony (un balcón) or a larger terrace (una terraza) and some also have a roof-top terrace (una azotea) where people can hang out their washing to dry. A Spanish pupil who travels in

to school from the outskirts (afueras) may live in a modern housing estate (urbanización).

Health and fitness

If you're ill, you might choose to go first to the chemist's (la farmacia) – look out for the sign in the shape of a green cross above the door. Here you can get advice and buy a wide range of medicines or antibiotics over the counter. If you need to see a doctor (un/a médico), you might go to a private consulting room (consulta) or to a health centre (centro de salud). If it's an emergency, you might be taken to the casualty department (urgencias) of the nearest hospital.

Food and drink

Every Spanish-speaking country has its own specialities, such as paella and sherry from Spain and tortillas and tacos from Mexico. In Spain, breakfast (el desayuno) is a light meal and lunch (el almuerzo) is the main meal of the day, usually eaten between half past one and three o'clock. A Spanish pupil might have a snack (merienda) around six or seven o'clock, and a light evening meal (cena) between nine and eleven o'clock.

You'll need to be able to talk in Spanish about what you eat and drink, and discuss your home and school life.
So let's get started – ¡vámonos!

InfoZONE

◎ These phrases will be really useful for your exam, so see if you can try and learn them!

School subjects

¿Cuántas asignaturas estudias?
How many subjects are you studying?

Estudio ... ocho.   I'm studying ... eight.

¿Cuáles son?   What are they?

Estudio inglés, francés, español, ciencias ...
I study English, French, Spanish, science ...

¿Qué asignaturas prefieres?
Which subjects do you prefer?

Me gusta la historia y me encantan las matemáticas.
I like history and I love maths.

¿Hay alguna asignatura que no te gusta?
Are there any subjects you don't like?

Odio ... la ética, porque es aburrida.
I hate ... PSE because it's boring.

The school day

¿Cómo vas al instituto?
How do you get to school?

Voy en autobús/a pie.   I go by bus/on foot.

Mi madre me lleva en coche.
My mother takes me in the car.

¿A qué hora empiezan las clases?
When do classes begin?

Empiezan a las nueve, y terminan a las tres.
They begin at nine and finish at three.

¿Cuántas clases hay al día?
How many classes are there a day?

Hay cinco.   There are five.

Life at home

¿Vives en una casa o un piso?
Do you live in a house or a flat?

Vivo en una casa antigua en las afueras.
I live in an old house on the outskirts.

En mi dormitorio, hay una cama, un armario ...   In my bedroom there's a bed, a cupboard ...

Me levanto a las siete.   I get up at seven.

Me baño o me ducho.
I have a bath or shower.

Me lavo/limpio los dientes.
I brush my teeth.

Me visto y me peino.
I get dressed and brush my hair.

Me acuesto ... a las once.
I go to bed ... at eleven.

Health and fitness

No me encuentro bien.   I don't feel well.

¿Qué te pasa?   What's the matter?

Me duele la cabeza.   I've got a headache.

Me duelen los ojos.   My eyes are sore.

Tengo fiebre.   I've got a temperature.

Hago deporte.   I do sport.

No fumo y no tomo drogas.
I don't smoke and I don't take drugs.

Food and drink

¿Qué tipo de comida te gusta?
What type of food do you like?

Me gusta ... el pescado.   I like ... fish.

No me gustan ... las zanahorias.
I don't like ... carrots.

la carne, las verduras, las legumbres
meat, green vegetables, (other) vegetables

las pastas, los pasteles, los postres
pasta, cakes, desserts

Soy vegetariano/a.   I'm a vegetarian.

Listening

When you're doing the listening activities in this book, don't try to watch the programme at the same time. You won't be able to follow what's happening on screen. The TV programme has the same section headings as this book. First of all, find the clip you need, play it through once and just watch. Then rewind the video to the start of the clip. Read the instruction for the activity, get your pencil ready, play the clip once more and do the activity in the book. If you like, you can listen through once again before checking your answers at the back of the book.

REMEMBER
It's a good idea to watch the clip one more time after you've checked your answers at the back of the book.

School subjects

Watch the Spanish pupils in the programme talking about which school subjects they study: **¿Qué asignaturas estudias?** You'll hear pupils on the programme calling Spanish both **español** and **lengua** (language). You can do the same when talking about English: **Estudio lengua y literatura** means 'I study (English) language and literature'.

REMEMBER
Your exam board will have its own list of picture symbols. Ask your teacher for a copy to help you learn to recognise them.

(?) First, look at the grid below. Which subjects are represented here? How many other school subjects can you name which aren't shown?

1 1066 1492 1918 1945	2 el mundo	3 ¡hola! ¡hola! ¡hola! ¡hola!	4 GB GB	5	6 23 +14 37	7	8

Now try the activity. You have to put a tick in the appropriate column each time a subject is mentioned – some subjects might not be mentioned at all.

(◎) **Escucha y escribe ✓ en la columna correcta.** Listen and put a ✓ in the correct column.

In the exam, you might also get some questions to answer in English. Find the clip where pupils answer the questions: **¿Qué asignatura prefieres?** and **¿Qué asignatura detestas?** and do the activity below.

(◎) **Escucha y contesta a las preguntas.** Listen and answer the questions.

1 Which science subject is liked?
2 Which subject is most disliked?

Daily routine

You'll almost certainly have to do an activity in which you decide whether statements are true (**verdad/verdaderas**) or false (**mentira/falsas**). There are different types of these, and you need to read the instructions carefully each time. You may be asked just to tick the statements which are correct or – as in the activity below – you might have to put a tick for each statement in either the true or the false column.

Find the clip in which Diana and Patricia talk about the first day of term, and do the activity below.

◎ **Escucha y escribe ✓ en la columna correcta.** Listen and put a ✓ in the correct column.

	Verdad	Mentira
Ejemplo: El profe nos llama dentro.	✓	☐
1 Hay asamblea en el salón de actos.	☐	☐
2 El profe pasa lista a los alumnos.	☐	☐
3 Nos dice el horario.	☐	☐
4 Estudiamos francés.	☐	☐
5 Hay clase de matemáticas.	☐	☐
6 Dibujamos la figura humana.	☐	☐
7 La hora de comer es el mejor momento del día.	☐	☐
8 Aprendemos las capitales de Europa.	☐	☐

> ❗ **REMEMBER**
> Where there is a true or a false column to tick, it's important not to leave any statement with two blank boxes. If you're really stuck, then have a guess: you've got a fifty-fifty chance of getting it right!

Sometimes you might be asked to complete sentences in Spanish. Don't be put off by this type of activity – you don't have to write more than a few words. You can try to work out the kind of words you might hear on the tape by carefully reading the beginnings of the sentences on the exam paper first. The title, if there is one, might also give you a clue as to what it's all going to be about.

⁇ For instance, read the beginnings of the five sentences below. For which of them do you think you might need to write down: a time, a room or place, a part of the body or the name of a person? The last word or two before the dotted line in each sentence will give you a clue.

Mi rutina
1 Me despierto y voy al ....
2 Me limpio ....
3 Me visto y juego con ....
4 Desayuno a las ....
5 Vuelvo de clase y como en ....

> ❗ **REMEMBER**
> Learn the Spanish for the 'little' words, like **a** (to, at), **en** (in, at), **con** (with), **de** (of, from), **y** (and), **pero** (but).

Now find the start of the clip about Noyer and Susana's day. Listen – stop before their visit to the television station, and do the activity below.

◎ **Escucha y completa las frases (1–5) en español.** Listen and complete the sentences (1–5 above) in Spanish.

House and home

In the exam, you might be asked to select the correct answer from alternatives. Make sure you read the sentences carefully first. Find the clip where Yimer and Alex explore Yimer's house, and do the activity below.

◎ **Escucha y subraya la(s) palabra(s) apropiada(s) para completar las frases 1–5.** Listen and underline the correct word(s) to complete each sentence.

1 La casa de Yimer es **pequeña/mediana/grande**.
2 Su casa es **nueva/antigua/fea**.
3 En total hay **6/7/8** *habitaciones.*
4 El salón es **muy/bastante/no muy** *grande.*
5 En la cocina hay una estufa **eléctrica/de gas**.

Intelligent guessing can be a help in exams, but it's not always enough. Trying to sit your exam without learning any words first is like trying to build a house without any bricks: you'll see why in a moment.

⑦ In the next activity, you have to listen and decide if the items a–f are in the dining room, the bedroom or the sitting room. Why can't you guess just by looking at the pictures?

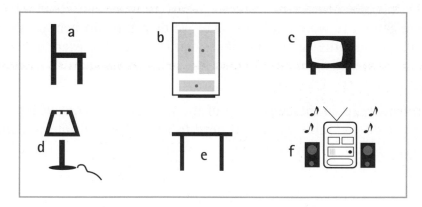

Because each item could be found in any of those three rooms, of course.

Now find the clip where Yimer shows you around his house in Popayán, and do the activity below.

◎ **Escucha y escribe las letras (a–f) en las casillas adecuadas.** Listen and write the letters (a–f) in the correct boxes.

1 En el comedor hay: ☐ ☐
2 En el dormitorio hay: ☐ ☐
3 En el salón hay: ☐ ☐

❗ REMEMBER Every listening activity you do is good practice for your exam. Ensure you make the best use of the opportunities your teacher gives you at school. You might be able to borrow a tape to listen to at home – do ask!

❗ REMEMBER Try and anticipate what words you might hear on the tape. Work out what you think the likely Spanish for each of the pictures might be. There might be more than one possibility, such as **mesa** (table) or **mesilla** (small table).

12

Places to eat

As well as general types of food, it will also help you in the exam to know a little about Spanish regional dishes. A popular starter, especially in the hot south in the summer, is **gazpacho**: a chilled soup made mainly from tomatoes and peppers. In the north, heavier dishes based around vegetables and pulses like lentils (**lentejas**) are a favourite. The rice dish **paella** comes from the Mediterranean coast in the east of Spain. Many people like to eat meat (**carne**), either as a fillet (**filete**) of lamb or pork, or in meat-based dishes like **cocido madrileño**, a stew from Madrid. Fish (**pescado**) is also very popular. Desserts are simple, with fruit and ice cream (**helado**) being favourite choices, as well as caramel custard (**flan**).

Now find the clip in which people are asked: **¿Qué te gusta tomar de primero/de segundo/de postre?** You need to listen carefully to their replies and decide which dishes they would be happy to eat from the menu below.

◉ Escucha y escribe ✓ al lado de los platos apropiados. Listen and put a ✓ beside the appropriate dishes.

❗ REMEMBER
When you're putting words or pictures in order, just scribble a number by each one as you hear it – then fill the answer in neatly on the exam paper. You can check your answer when you hear the recording a second time.

~ De primero ~	~ De segundo ~	~ De postre ~
Gazpacho	**Filete de cerdo**	**Flan** ....
Ensalada	**Pescado frito**	**Helados variados** ....
Lentejas con jamón	**Tortilla francesa o española**	**Fruta del tiempo** ....

Practice activity

As you revise, you'll probably make notes for yourself, write down useful words and collect model texts or recordings to learn from. It's a good idea to have all these things together safely somewhere, so you can find them easily whenever you want to revise Spanish. Get a file or a folder for yourself first of all. As you revise over the next few weeks, you can collect useful information in it and you can refer back to it for checking things or revising points again. Start your file off by writing a list of all your GCSE exam subjects – in Spanish of course!

You heard quite a lot of 'food' words in this programme, so now would be a good time to gather some of them together to collect in your Spanish revision file.

Start off by playing the section **En la hamburguesería** through once and noting down any food or drink words you hear – don't stop the clip at all as you listen. How many words can you pick out? Now listen again in more detail to pick the words out. There are quite a lot of food and drink words in it, so concentrate really hard and see how many you can spot. Write your words down on a piece of paper or record them on to a tape for future reference.

14

! REMEMBER The more often you see words, the easier they are to learn. Stick up your list of question words in Spanish and in English wherever you clean your teeth, and learn them as you brush!

At home and school

◎ You'll need to ask as well as answer questions in the exam, so see if you can match up the Spanish and the English for these question words.

1 ¿cuándo?	a) at what time?
2 ¿quién?	b) how?
3 ¿dónde?	c) who?
4 ¿qué?	d) when?
5 ¿cómo?	e) what?
6 ¿cuál?	f) how much?
7 ¿a qué hora?	g) where to?
8 ¿por qué?	h) which?
9 ¿adónde?	i) where?
10 ¿cuánto?	j) why?

?

?

(?) **¿Cómo es ...?** can also mean 'What is ... like?' For example: **¿Cómo es tu casa?** (What's your house like?) Can you work out how to ask a Spanish person: What's your school/garden/bedroom like?

◎ **Rellena los huecos.** Fill in the gaps.

1 Where is the bathroom?	¿........................ está el cuarto de baño?
2 At what time is dinner?	¿........................ está la cena?
3 When can I phone home?	¿........................ puedo llamar a casa?
4 Which is my towel?	¿........................ es mi toalla?
5 How much is a stamp for Great Britain?	¿........................ cuesta un sello para Gran Bretaña?
6 How do you say 'letter box' in Spanish?	¿........................ se dice 'letter box' en español?

! REMEMBER Even if you're allowed a dictionary to help you prepare before the speaking part of the exam, you won't have much time to look up words, so learning vocabulary now is vital!

It's very important to listen for the question word at the start of the sentence in the conversation part of the exam – if you don't understand it correctly, you may answer a question you haven't been asked and lose marks. For example, the difference between **¿Qué comes al mediodía?** and **¿Dónde comes al mediodía?** is that the first one asks you *what* you eat at lunchtime and the second asks *where* you eat – the question word is very important.

◎ **Contesta a las preguntas en español.** Answer the questions in Spanish.

1 ¿A qué hora te levantas?	(Me levanto ...)
2 ¿Qué desayunas?	(Desayuno ...)
3 ¿Cómo vas al instituto?	(Voy ...)
4 ¿Cuánto tiempo tardas en llegar?	(Tardo ...)
5 ¿Cuándo empiezan las clases?	(Empiezan ...)
6 ¿Dónde comes al mediodía?	(Como ...)
7 ¿Cuál es tu asignatura favorita?	(Prefiero ...)
8 ¿A qué hora terminan las clases?	(Terminan ...)

Food and drink

In the exam, you might well have to say when you do things, such as when you have meals. To say 'a.m.', use **de la mañana** (in the morning) and to say 'p.m.', use **de la tarde** (in the afternoon/evening) or **de la noche** (at night – usually after ten o'clock).

◎ Can you say the following times in Spanish?

7.00a.m.   8.30a.m.   11.00a.m.   1.30p.m.   6.00p.m.   10.30p.m.

In the exam, you might have to explain to a Spanish friend about mealtimes, so have a go at this activity.

◎ **Explica las horas de las comidas en español.** Explain the times of meals in Spanish.

Breakfast	7.30a.m.	(Desayuno ...)
Lunch	12.30p.m.	(Como/Almuerzo ...)
Snack	4.15p.m.	(Meriendo ...)
Evening meal	6.30p.m.	(Ceno ...)

◎ Mealtimes can be flexible and the expressions below will help make your conversation more interesting. Try explaining in Spanish when your own mealtimes are. Use at least two of these expressions:

a (las ocho) en punto	at (8.00) on the dot
a eso de (la una)	about (1.00)
entre (las seis) y (las seis y media)	between (6.00) and (6.30)

📺 In the exam, you might also have to order food and drink in a café or restaurant. There are lots of ways of saying what you want: **quiero ...,** **quisiera ..., voy a tomar ...** and **para mí ...** If you'd like to try something, you can say: **Me gustaría probar ...**

◎ **Explica lo que quieres comer y beber.** Explain what you want to eat and drink.

CAMARERO/A:	Buenas noches, señor. ¿Qué va a tomar?
TÚ:	De primero plato, quiero ....
CAMARERO/A:	¿Y de segundo?
TÚ:	Me gustaría probar ...
CAMARERO/A:	¿Y de postre?
TÚ:	Para mí ...
CAMARERO/A:	¿Y para beber?
TÚ:	Quisiera ...
CAMARERO/A:	En seguida.

tomato salad

Spanish omelette and chips

strawberry ice cream

fizzy mineral water

❓ Think up some more restaurant dialogues of your own. What other items of food and drink do you know?

! R E M E M B E R Use **a la una** for 'at one o'clock' and **a las ...** before other times: **a las seis** – 'at six o'clock'. Go to the BITESIZE website to find out more about telling the time in Spanish. 🔊

! R E M E M B E R In Spanish, **comer** means 'to eat' (in general), but also 'to have lunch'. You can use either **como** or **almuerzo** to mean 'I have lunch'.

! R E M E M B E R Try working through the BITESIZE material with a friend sometimes – it helps to have someone to practise with.

Speaking

Feeling ill

If you're feeling ill, you'll need to know the words for the parts of the body so you can explain what's wrong with you.

(?) How many of these parts of the body can you complete and say?

1 la cab--- (head)
2 la boc- (mouth)
3 la espal-- (back)
4 la ma-- (hand)
5 la pie--- (leg)

6 la nar-- (nose)
7 la garg---- (throat)
8 el bra-- (arm)
9 el estóm--- (stomach)
10 el pi- (foot)

When you want to explain that something hurts, use **me duele (el/la ...)** if one thing is hurting and **me duelen (los/las ...)** if it's more than one: **Me duele la garganta** (my throat hurts)/**Me duelen las manos** (my hands hurt).

(?) Using **me duele** or **me duelen**, explain that these things are hurting.

los ojos   la muñeca   los oídos   el hombro   los pies   la muela

You might have to do a role-play at the doctor's. The 'doctor' might start by asking how you are (**¿Qué tal estás?**), then what's the matter (**¿Qué te pasa?**), how long you've been unwell (**¿Desde hace cuánto tiempo no te sientes bien?**) and if you have other symptoms (**¿Tienes otros síntomas?**).

(◎) **Sustituye las expresiones subrayadas por otras apropiadas.** Replace the underlined expressions with other ones. Make up two dialogues.

– ¿Qué tal?
– *No me encuentro bien.*
– ¿Qué te pasa?
– Me duele *la garganta*.
– ¿Desde hace cuánto tiempo no te sientes bien?
– *Desde ayer.*
– ¿Tienes otros síntomas?
– Tengo *catarro* también.
– Vamos a ver ...

> la cabeza
> no me siento bien
> desde hace dos días
> no estoy muy bien
> el estómago
> naúseas
> fiebre
> desde anoche

Practice activity

It's easy to practise speaking Spanish. You can say words out loud or in your head whenever you want to – just to get used to the sounds and feel comfortable with saying them. Next time you're walking to the shops, waiting for a bus or even having a bath, look around you – what can you see? Try and say some of the words in Spanish – you can either say single words or try to make up a whole sentence or a question with them.

GrammarZONE

You will have noticed that there are lots of words for 'the' in Spanish. There are actually four: **el, la, los** and **las**. In Spanish, all nouns (objects, places, people) are either masculine (m) or feminine (f). They can also be singular (s), meaning there's one of them or plural (pl), meaning there's more than one of them.

m (s)	f (s)	m (pl)	f (pl)
el libro	la pluma	los libros	las plumas
(the book)	(the pen)	(the books)	(the pens)

If you're not sure whether a Spanish word is masculine or feminine, you can look it up in a dictionary or the wordlist at the back of your textbook. Be careful though – not all words which end in the letter 's' are plural.

◎ Write **el, la, los** or **las** before each of the following words.

.... regla .... sacapuntas .... goma .... compás
.... cuadernos .... bolígrafo .... mochila .... carpetas

Do you know how people talk about liking and disliking things? Can you work out from the sentences below when to use **gusta** and when to use **gustan**?

Me gusta el dibujo. ♥
Me gustan mucho las ciencias. ♥♥
No me gustan las matemáticas. ✗
No me gusta nada la historia. ✗✗

You use **gusta** with singular nouns (**el, la**) and **gustan** with plural nouns (**los, las**).

◎ Put **gusta** or **gustan** in each of the gaps below.

1 No me .... la física.
2 Me .... las verduras.
3 El deporte no me ....
4 Me .... los trabajos manuales.
5 ¿Te .... el café?
6 ¿Los deberes? ¡No me .... nada!

⁇ What do you notice about the words coming after **gusta** in the following opinions?

Me gusta jugar al fútbol. *¿No te gusta leer?* *Me gusta salir al cine.*

The words **jugar, leer** and **salir** are all verbs in their infinitive form: they end in **-ar, -er** or **-ir**. When using a verb after **gusta**, it will be in the infinitive form.

◎ Match up the two halves of the following sentences correctly.

1 Me gusta mucho ver la ...	a los concursos: son estúpidos.
2 No me gustan ...	b deporte, sobre todo el fútbol.
3 Me gusta ...	c noticias, porque son aburridas.
4 Me gusta el ...	d escuchar discos compactos.
5 No me gustan nada las ...	e televisión – hay programas interesantes.

! REMEMBER Take the time to read the introductory sentence or the title on an activity, if there is one. It sets the scene and can help you focus on what to do.

School

The first tasks in your reading exam might ask you to answer questions in English. You may feel these will be very easy, but this is not always so. They often test whether you know basic things like the time, numbers and days of the week – and, as examiners point out every year, mistakes are made more often than you might think.

(?) Can you say all the days of the week, starting with Sunday and working back to Monday? What's the difference between **dos, doce, veintidós** and **doscientos**?

Now test yourself with this activity where you're on an exchange visit to Spain. You read this notice on the door into school.

◎ **Lee y contesta a las preguntas.** Read and answer the questions.

! REMEMBER Make sure you understand the Spanish instructions for activities. Ask your teacher for a list of the ones used by your exam board, then learn them, just like you would any other vocabulary.

1 On which day does the event take place?
2 Which floor do you have to go to?
3 Are you invited to:
    a a dance
    b eat something
    c attend an English class?
4 How much does it cost to go?
    a 120 pesetas
    b 220 pesetas
    c 200 pesetas

> **ALUMNOS DEL INTERCAMBIO**
> **(ESPAÑA – INGLATERRA)**
> Merienda con churros
> Aula 5, planta baja
> Miércoles, 16.00
> ¡Sólo doscientas pesetas!

In another type of reading activity, you may have to match up sentences and pictures. Don't reach for your dictionary when you come across the first word you don't know. First, study all the pictures carefully – what are they? What word(s) does each one suggest to you? Then read the text and see if you can find words which relate to the pictures. Have a go at the following activity.

! REMEMBER Check whether you need to match up all of the sentences and pictures – sometimes there is one which will be left over.

◎ **Empareja los anuncios con los símbolos.** Match the announcements to the pictures.

1 Semana de la Salud, mayo 7–14: ¡venid al instituto a pie!
2 ¿Te interesa visitar Gran Bretaña? Octubre 15–22, viaje en avión.
3 Autocar Centro-Río Rosas. Salida 14.40.
4 ¡Perdido! Permiso de tren. Ana Vallejas 1ºEGB.
5 ¡Si vienes en moto, hay que llevar casco!
6 Nuevo – soporte para bicicletas, detrás del gimnasio.

Eating out

You will also have reading activities to do which are only in Spanish. The layout of the task and the example (**ejemplo**) will help to show you what to do. Try the following activity where you see a menu in a restaurant window.

¿Qué se puede comer? Escribe ✓ en las 3 casillas adecuadas. What can you eat? Put a ✓ in the 3 correct boxes.

✓

Ejemplo: sopa ☐
1 *pescado* ☐
2 *carne* ☐
3 *huevos* ☐
4 *legumbres* ☐
5 *helados* ☐
6 *fruta* ☐

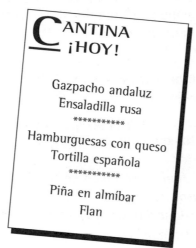

C ANTINA ¡HOY!

Gazpacho andaluz
Ensaladilla rusa
****

Hamburguesas con queso
Tortilla española
****

Piña en almíbar
Flan

REMEMBER
If the instruction asks you to tick three boxes, do tick three, even if you're not sure of all your answers – you can't get any marks for leaving a blank space. The example does not count as one of them.

You might have a form to complete in Spanish after reading a brief description. You don't need to write full sentences on the form, but you should write clearly. Always read the text with care first: there's often more than one way of expressing something.

For example, how many ways can you think of to convey likes and preferences? See if you can spot four ways in Ben's note below.

Hola,
¡Me llamo Ben! ¿Qué tipo de comida me gusta? Pues, ¡varios! Me gustan las pastas – macarrones, espaguetis, lasaña – en salsa de tomate con queso. Pero no tomo ni pescado ni carne. Me encantan los huevos, sobre todo la tortilla española. Las verduras y las ensaladas son muy buenas también. Pero odio el colifor: es algo que no aguanto. En cuanto a bebidas, prefiero el zumo de fruta – pero no bebo café.

REMEMBER
Only write down the information you are asked to give. You may not get any marks for writing down lots of items when you're only asked for one.

Rellena el formulario para Ben. Complete the form for Ben.

1 Nombre: _____
2 Comida preferida: _____
3 Detesta: _____
4 Le gusta beber: _____
5 ¿Vegetariano/a?: (dibujo un círculo) Sí/No

Routines

You might have to match questions to answers – and there might be a spare answer. Remember that you don't need to understand every word and the question words themselves can often give you a clue. For instance, if you see a question beginning: **¿A qué hora ...?**, you can be fairly sure that the answer will include a time. Have you learnt the question words yet? If not, go back to page 14 and refresh your memory before tackling this activity.

R E M E M B E R In matching activities, always do the ones you're really sure of first, and then look at any ones left over.

◎ **Empareja las preguntas 1–6 con las respuestas a–f.** Match the questions 1–6 with the answers a–f.

1 *¿Dónde está tu instituto?*
2 *¿Cuántos alumnos hay en tu instituto?*
3 *¿A qué hora pasan lista en tu instituto?*
4 *¿Qué asignatura no te gusta?*
5 *¿Dónde almuerzas a mediodía?*
6 *¿Tienes muchos deberes?*

a *Vuelvo a casa para comer.*
b *Unos mil quinientos.*
c *Está en el centro de la ciudad.*
d *A las nueve de la mañana.*
e *Por lo menos dos horas al día.*
f *Odio la biología.*

| 1C | | | | | |

Don't be put off by longer pieces of text! You might have to read a short paragraph and then decide which of the sentences about it are correct.

R E M E M B E R You need to be familiar with the 24-hour clock. Every time you look at your watch or a clock for the next 24 hours, try and say the time in Spanish. Remember: half past three is the same as fifteen thirty.

❓ Below are six sentences about Nuria's day. Read them first and check you understand them. Watch out for small words like **no** in number 2. When is **mediodía** and **las catorce treinta**?

1 *El colegio es pequeño.* ☐
2 *No le gustan las matemáticas.* ☐
3 *Estudia nueve asignaturas en total.* ☐
4 *Le gusta el profesor de historia.* ☐
5 *Hay un recreo de quince minutos al mediodía.* ☐
6 *Las clases terminan a las catorce treinta.* ☐

◎ **Lee la carta de Nuria. Escribe ✓ al lado de las 4 frases correctas.** Read Nuria's letter. Put a ✓ beside the 4 correct sentences above.

Mi colegio es bastante grande: tiene 900 alumnos. Estudio literatura, geografía, historia, matemáticas, ciencias, deporte, francés y ética. Mi asignatura favorita es el deporte. Odio las matemáticas – ¡y tengo dos horas seguidas los jueves! Pero la historia es muy interesante porque el profesor es bueno. Las clases empiezan a las ocho y media, y terminan a las dos y media. Hay un recreo de quince minutos a las doce – ¡menos mal!

Staying healthy

You might get several texts written by different people to read. You will then have to decide to which person some statements refer. Run your eye down each text below. Which words do you recognise? What are the texts about?

(?) Read through the accounts of these young adults. Do they mention: eating, feeling ill, drinking, sport, drug-taking, school, chores, smoking?

Soy muy deportista. Hago footing dos veces a la semana, y voy a la piscina el sábado. No bebo alcohol – es malo para la salud. Muchos de mis amigos fuman pero yo no. En cuanto a la comida, sigo un régimen sano. Siempre desayuno, almuerzo en la cantina de la fábrica y por la tarde, ceno fruta y yogur.

JOAQUÍN

¡Yo estoy fatal! Soy adicto al chocolate (dos tabletas cada día), a los cigarillos (cinco cada día) y no tomo nunca ejercicio. Pero no tomo drogas. Todos los días, me digo que voy a cambiar, que voy a hacer ejercicio y comer bien – pero no lo hago.

PACO

Yo me cuido bien. Me levanto temprano todos los días para hacer yoga, y voy al trabajo andando. Nunca uso el coche entresemana. El fin de semana, me gusta salir de la ciudad e ir a la montaña de paseo. Tomo un poco de vino con la cena cada noche, pero aparte de eso, no bebo.

ALICIA

(!) **R E M E M B E R**
The more you read in Spanish, the easier and quicker it is to 'get the gist' of an article. Ask your teacher if he or she has got any Spanish magazines you can borrow, or the addresses of any useful Internet sites. Don't forget the BBC BITESIZE site. The address is on the back of this book.

(◎) Para cada frase 1–6, escribe el nombre de la persona apropiada (Joaquín, Paco, Alicia). For each sentence 1–6, write the name of the appropriate person (Joaquín, Paco, Alicia).

1 Le gusta ir a pie al trabajo. ....
2 Fuma bastante. ....
3 Toma ejercicio físico todos los días. ....
4 Come bien. ....
5 No bebe nunca. ....
6 Es muy perezoso/a. ....

Practice activity

Here's a practice question for you to try. The instruction is given to you only in Spanish this time.

(◎) Lee la información de la Teleguía. Para cada programa 1–5, escribe la hora correcta.

Ejemplo: el tiempo   19.00
1 deporte   ....
2 telenovela   ....
3 película de amor/acción   ....
4 concurso   ....
5 dibujos animados   ....

17.00	Cuentos de Walt Disney
17.30	Farmacia de Guardia (Episodio 100)
18.00	Baloncesto (Barcelona – Zaragoza)
19.00	Telediario y Meteo
20.00	Cine: Titanic
22.30	321 – ¡Premios a ganar!
23.20	Debate

Writing

Your bedroom

📺 In the programme clip from Popayán, you see Yimer talking about his bedroom. You may well have to describe your bedroom in the exam, too. What kind of things have you got in it?

◎ **Completa el rompecabezas.** Complete the furniture puzzle by writing in the vowels (a, e, i, o, u).

1 You sleep in this!					C		M		
2 Useful for hanging things in.	G		R	D		R	R		P
3 A floor is cold without this.		L	F		M	B	R		
4 Good for putting books on.			S	T		N	T		
5 Every room has at least one!	P				R	T			
6 Useful to have beside the bed.	M		S		L	L			
7 Should have plenty of drawers.	C		M		D				

8 You can put lots of things in this!

REMEMBER Masculine words (**un**) are marked (m) in the dictionary and feminine ones (**una**) are marked (f).

❓ When making a list of things in your room, you'll need to write the Spanish for 'a' (**un/una**). Can you remember which to put in front of each of the items above? Use your dictionary if you need to.

Now try this exam type question where you need to write a list of some bedroom items. Try to include at least five items which are not in the puzzle above (e.g. lamp, stereo, picture).

◎ **Escribe una lista de 8 artículos de tu dormitorio.** Write a list of 8 items from your bedroom.

Ejemplo	un póster
1	
2	
3	
4	
5	
6	
7	
8	

Your home

In the exam, it's likely that you will have an opportunity to write about your home. You will earn more marks for quality of language if you can describe it fully. Adjectives like 'old', 'big' and 'pretty' add interest to a description.

(?) First, read the information about Miguel's home below. How many adjectives (describing words) does he use?

> Vivo en una casa[1] en el centro de la ciudad. Tiene siete habitaciones: una entrada[2], una cocina[3], un salón-comedor[4], un cuarto de baño[5] y tres dormitorios. Hay una terraza[6] con flores.

He doesn't use any adjectives at all!

(?) Now see if you can use each of the adjectives a–f below after each of the nouns 1–6 in Miguel's letter. If the noun is feminine (**una**), then its adjective has to be feminine too: **Vivo en un̲a cas̲a antigu̲a**.

a antiguo/a (old)   d grande (big)
b pequeño/a (small)   e espacioso/a (spacious)
c nuevo/a (new)   f bonito/a (pretty)

Miguel's letter doesn't explain where things are. You might find the following phrases useful when trying to make a description more interesting.

(◎) **Empareja las frases.** Match the expressions.

1 a la izquierda   a downstairs
2 a la derecha   b which opens on to the terrace
3 al fondo   c upstairs
4 arriba   d on the left
5 abajo   e altogether/in total
6 que da a la terraza   f at the end/back/rear
7 en total   g on the right

(?) Now try and write a full description of Miguel's house. Use the plan, the words above and the description you completed. You could start: **Vivo en una casa antigua en el centro de la ciudad. Tiene siete ...**

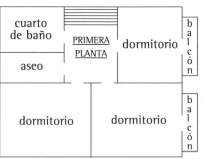

Now use everything you have learnt on this page to write a description of your own home: try to keep the examiner interested!

(◎) **Describe tu casa.** Write a description of your home.

! REMEMBER Use your notes from class or a dictionary to remind yourself of other useful words you know, as well as the ones from BITESIZE. What's the Spanish for cloakroom, utility room, study, attic ...?

! REMEMBER Check your spelling when you've finished against the words here on the page. Look at every word very carefully. Correct any which are wrong, and write them out three times correctly on a spare piece of paper.

Writing

Household chores

You might be given a sample letter to read and reply to in the exam, for example about jobs you do around the house. At least writing about them is not as bad as having to do them. Read Miguel's letter below.

◎ **Rellena los blancos correctamente.** Fill in the gaps correctly.

> ¡*Entre semana*, todo el mundo tiene que hacer algo! *Todos los días* tengo que **(1)**...................... mi habitación y hacer la cama. ¡Qué aburrido! Tengo que poner la mesa, y ayudar a **(2)**...................... la comida *dos veces a la semana*. Mi hermana Julia tiene que **(3)**...................... el suelo de la cocina y sacar la basura. *El viernes por la noche* vamos todos al supermercado para **(4)**...................... la compra. *El fin de semana* hay mucho que hacer. Mi padre tiene que **(5)**...................... la ropa y yo ayudo a planchar. *El domingo* mi hermana suele **(6)**...................... la aspiradora y ayuda a regar las plantas. ¿Y tú? ¿Qué tienes que hacer en casa para ayudar?

hacer
preparar
lavar
arreglar
barrer
pasar

◎ In Miguel's letter there are another five chores mentioned. Can you underline them?

◎ It will make your writing more interesting if you can say how often you and others in your family have to do chores. In Miguel's letter, can you find the Spanish for the following expressions?

1 on Friday night ....
2 every day ....
3 at the weekend ....
4 twice a week ....
5 on Sunday ....

You'll need to say who has to do what in your family and the following expressions are useful for this:

Explaining what you do		Explaining what other people do	
Tengo que ...	I have to ...	*Mi (padre) tiene que ...*	My (father) has to ...
Ayudo a ...	I help to ...	*Mi (hermano) ayuda a ...*	My (brother) helps to ...
Suelo ...	I usually ...	*Mi (hermana) suele ...*	My (sister) usually ...

These expressions can all be used with the infinitive of the verb: **tengo que hac<u>er</u> la cama/Julia tiene que sac<u>ar</u> la basura**.

◎ Can you now explain who does what in your house? Write down six sentences starting with an expression above: **Tengo que poner la mesa**.

You can use Miguel's letter as a model for this next activity. Don't forget to say what other members of your family do.

◎ **¿Qué tienes que hacer en casa para ayudar?** What do you have to do at home to help?

REMEMBER
Things you prepare for the writing exam can often be used in the speaking exam presentation and conversation section as well. Make your work work for you!

REMEMBER
If you want to explain that you don't do something, put **no** before the **tengo/tiene, ayudo/ ayuda** and **suelo/suele**.

Media: television and the cinema

If you're aiming for a higher grade in the exam, then you need to give your opinion on things.

◎ Look at these adjectives. Which are positive and which are negative?

1 interesante(s)	6 bueno/a(s)
2 aburrido/a(s)	7 estúpido/a(s)
3 divertido/a(s)	8 pesado/a(s)
4 malo/a(s)	9 tonto/a(s)
5 estupendo/a(s)	10 emocionante(s)

Do you remember about making adjectives agree? Check whether the films below are masculine (**los**) or feminine (**las**) and put the correct ending on the adjective; don't forget to add an **-s**: <u>Los</u> westerns son aburrid<u>os</u>.

◎ **Completa las opiniones de Arantxa.** Complete Arantxa's opinions. Use the adjectives (1–10) above.

Creo que las películas románticas son (7) ....
¿Los dibujos animados? Son (9) ....
Las comedias son (3) ....
En mi opinión, las películas de ciencia-ficción son (10) ....
Los programas deportivos son (6) ....
Pienso que las películas de aventuras son (5) ....

Arantxa used other expressions for giving an opinion: **creo que** and **pienso que** both mean 'I think that' and **en mi opinión** means 'in my opinion'.

⑦ See if you can give your own opinion of the following types of films.

las películas de terror	*las noticias*
las películas históricas	*los concursos*
las películas policíacas	*las telenovelas*

You might have to write about going to the cinema (**fui al cine**), or a film you've seen (**vi** 'I saw'), and give your opinion. Talking about the best (**lo mejor**) or the worst thing (**lo peor**) adds colour to your writing. You could choose **la música** (music), **el humor** (humour), **el ambiente** (atmosphere), **el/la protagonista** (main character) or **los efectos especiales** (special effects).

Practice activity

Write a short paragraph about films you like and dislike. Include a brief account of a film you've seen recently on TV (**en la televisión**) or in the cinema. Use the adjectives and phrases above. Here are some more useful expressions to help you:

Me gustan/encantan ...	*No me gustan/odio ...*
Fui al cine (el sábado pasado)	*Vi una película de acción 'Armageddon'*
Fue/era muy (emocionante)	*Lo mejor/peor fue (la música).*

❗ REMEMBER You can use these 'opinion' words with other topics too, such as school subjects, chores, sports and hobbies, holidays ...

❗ REMEMBER Try to use words like **fui** (I went), **vi** (I saw) and **era** (it was) to show the examiner you can talk about the past as well as the present.

Personal Life

This section is about

- Family and friends

- Interests and hobbies

- Special occasions

- Arranging to go out

- Pocket money

This section is all about your personal life, and that includes talking about your appearance and personality, your family and pets, your hobbies and free-time activities, pocket money and going out, and special occasions you celebrate in your family or community.

Family and friends

In Spain, everyone has two surnames: the first one is the father's surname, and the second is the mother's. Family life is very strong: many young people continue to live at home while they go to further education courses at college or university, and they might not leave home until they get married or get their first job. Grandparents and older relatives often live with or near the family, and they are cared for by them.

Interests and hobbies

The most popular spectator sport in the Spanish-speaking world is football (**el fútbol**). Basketball (**el baloncesto**) is also widely played in Spain and baseball (**el beisbol**) in South America. Another popular sport in the north of Spain is the Basque **pelota** (**el jai-alai** in Mexico) a game like squash. Bull-fighting (**la corrida de toros**) continues to have dedicated audiences across Spanish-speaking countries.

Special occasions

Sometimes it seems as if there's a 'fiesta' every day! At baptism, children are also given the name of a saint, and the celebration of this saint's day (**el santo**) is as important as their birthday (**el cumpleaños**). Every town or village has a patron saint (**el santo patrón**) whose feast day is an occasion for music and dancing. Many festivals are religious in origin: Holy Week (**la Semana Santa**) is celebrated with great solemnity, and cities like Seville are famous for their torchlit processions of floats (**pasos**) depicting scenes from the life of Jesus. The Three Kings (**los Reyes Magos**) leave presents and sweets in children's shoes on January 6th.

Arranging to go out and pocket money

Going to the cinema (**el cine**), the pool (**la piscina**) or the sports centre (**el polideportivo**) are favourite pastimes with teenagers, who often go round in large groups of friends (**pandillas**) – just 'hanging out' (**ir por ahí**) is also popular. It's not always easy to find part-time work in Spain, but some teenagers may work in the family business in the holidays. In poorer areas of South America, money earned by children is needed to pay for food, clothes and schooling for the family or community. So let's get started – **¡vámonos!**

◎ These phrases will be really useful for your exam, so see if you can try and learn them!

Family and friends

¿Cuántas personas hay en tu familia?
How many people are there in your family?

Somos ... cuatro.   There are ... four of us.

¿Quiénes son?   Who are they?

Mi madre, mi padrastro, mi hermana y yo.
My mother, my step-father, my sister and me.

¿Cómo es tu físico?   What do you look like?

Soy alto/a y bastante delgado/a.
I'm tall and quite slim.

Tengo el pelo corto y marrón.
I've got short brown hair.

Tengo los ojos azules.   I've got blue eyes.

De carácter, ¿cómo eres?
What kind of person are you?

Soy alegre y amable, pero un poco perezoso/a.
I'm cheerful and kind, but a bit lazy.

Interests and hobbies

¿Qué deportes practicas?
What sports do you play?

Juego al baloncesto y practico la gimnasia.
I play basketball and I do gymnastics.

Soy miembro del equipo de natación.
I'm a member of the swimming team.

¿Qué otras cosas te gustan hacer?
What other things do you like to do?

Toco la guitarra y aprendo el tai-chi.
I play the guitar and I'm learning tai-chi.

Me gusta salir con mis amigos.
I like going out with my friends.

El fin de semana voy a la pista de hielo.
At the weekend I go to the ice-rink.

Special occasions

¿Cómo celebras el cumpleaños?
How do you celebrate your birthday?

Invito a unos amigos y hacemos una fiesta.
I invite friends and we have a party.

¿Qué otras fiestas se celebran en tu familia?
What other festivals do you celebrate in your family?

Celebramos la Navidad/el Año Nuevo/Divali.
We celebrate Christmas/New Year/Divali.

Enviamos tarjetas, y compramos regalos.
We send cards and buy presents.

Adornamos .... un pino/la casa.
We decorate ... a tree/the house.

Nos reunimos para una comida especial.
We get together for a special meal.

Vamos ... a la iglesia/a la mezquita.
We go ....to church/to the mosque.

Arranging to go out and pocket money

¿Te gustaría ... salir?
Would you like to ... go out?

Me gustaría .... ir al cine.
I'd like to ... go to the cinema.

Lo siento, no puedo. No tengo tiempo.
I'm sorry, I can't. I haven't got time.

¿A qué hora/dónde nos vemos?
When/where shall we meet?

Enfrente de Correos, a las siete.
Opposite the post office, at seven.

¿Te dan dinero tus padres?
Do your parents give you money?

Me dan dos libras a la semana/al mes.
I get two pounds a week/a month.

Hago tareas en casa para ganar dinero.
I do jobs at home to earn money.

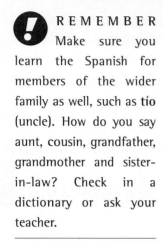

Listening

Introductions and interviews

When listening to introductions, you will usually hear the name (**nombre**) of the person introduced and some other information about her or him, such as: **Éste es mi amigo, Raúl** (this is my friend, Raúl) or: **Ésta es mi hermana, Mercedes** (this is my sister, Mercedes).

(?) How many other Spanish words for family members can you list in one minute? Here are some to get you started: **padre** (father), **tío** (uncle).

Now listen to Isabel introducing her family and try this first activity.

◎ Escucha y completa las frases. Listen and complete the sentences.

1 *Ésta es mi* ...., *María.*
2 *Éste es mi* ...., *Paco.*
3 *Ésa es Ana, mi* ....
4 *Ése es Miguel, mi* ....

> hermanastro, hermano, padrastro, hermana, madrastra, padre, madre, hermanastro

(?) What's the English for each of the words left over from the box?

Did you notice how to say 'this is ...' and 'that is ...'? You need **éste** (this) and **ése** (that) for males; use **ésta** (this) and **ésa** (that) for females.

(?) How would you introduce the members of your family? For example: **Ésta es mi madrastra, Claire** (this is my step-mother, Claire).

Now find the clip where Diana introduces her family, and try the activity below.

◎ Escucha y rellena la ficha con los detalles que faltan. Listen and complete the form with the missing details.

1 Nombre: Diana

2 Apellido: del Olmo Saugar

3 Edad: 12 años

4 Número de personas en casa:

5 Número de hermanos:

6 Número de hermanas:

7 Animales (tipo):

! REMEMBER Make sure you learn the Spanish for members of the wider family as well, such as **tío** (uncle). How do you say aunt, cousin, grandfather, grandmother and sister-in-law? Check in a dictionary or ask your teacher.

! REMEMBER Other words for 'address' on forms include **señas** and **dirección**.

Describing yourself

You'll need to get used to hearing people from different parts of Spain and other Spanish-speaking countries and communities, as you may hear them in the exam. You'll probably have heard, and learnt, your pronunciation mostly from Spanish speakers living in Spain. However, in South America, for instance, some letters are pronounced differently. You'll be used to hearing speakers from Spain saying the letter '**z**' as a '**th**' sound, just like the letter '**c**' when followed by an '**e**' or an '**i**': die<u>z</u> is pronounced as '**die<u>th</u>**' and <u>c</u>inco as '**<u>th</u>inko**'. However, in South American Spanish both these sounds are pronounced as an '**s**': '**die<u>s</u>**' and '**<u>s</u>inko**'.

Now listen to a group of young people from Colombia. Find the clip which begins just after Carolina, Eduar, Sarita and Yimer have introduced themselves. Remember what you've read above about the letter '**th**' and the letter '**c**' when followed by an '**e**' or an '**i**'.

◎ **Escucha y completa las frases.** Listen and complete the sentences.

YIMER: *Mi nombre es Yimer Álvarez.*
CAROLINA: *Vivo en Popayán, Colombia, América Latina.*
SARITA: *Tengo .... años.*
EDUAR: *Tengo .... años.*
CAROLINA: *Tengo .... años.*
              Mi cumpleaños es el veintitrés de ....
EDUAR: *Mi cumpleaños es el treinta de agosto.*

Not only can the pronunciation be different, but some of the vocabulary is too. In Spain, people use the word **pelo** for hair, but in South America you'll hear **cabello**. The colour 'brown', to describe hair, is **marrón** in Spain and sometimes **café** in South American Spanish. Listen carefully to the next section, where the reporters describe themselves, and do the activity below.

◎ **Para cada descripción escribe el nombre de la persona adecuada.** For each description write the name of the appropriate person: Carolina, Eduar, Sarita or Yimer.

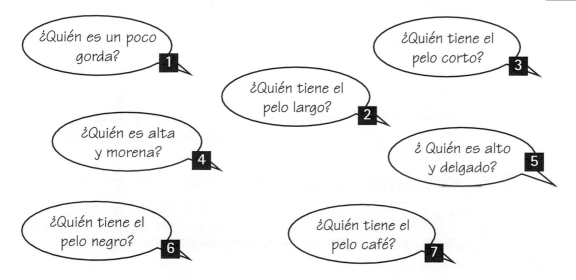

¿Quién es un poco gorda? **1**

¿Quién tiene el pelo largo? **2**

¿Quién tiene el pelo corto? **3**

¿Quién es alta y morena? **4**

¿Quién es alto y delgado? **5**

¿Quién tiene el pelo negro? **6**

¿Quién tiene el pelo café? **7**

REMEMBER Listening to as much Spanish as you can will really make a difference to your listening skills. You might be able to borrow tapes from your school or local library, or even access Spanish and South American programmes on satellite television.

REMEMBER South America is known as both **América del Sur** and **América Latina**. Somebody who describes themselves as South American would be called **sudamericano/a**.

Free time

In the exam, you might have to listen for details and match them to the appropriate pictures. Find the clip in which the interviewer begins with the question: **¿Qué te gusta hacer en tu tiempo libre?** and listen to the replies of the first five people he interviews. Then, study the grid of sports and hobbies below and try the following activity as you listen again.

! R E M E M B E R
The verb **jugar** is irregular. Use **me gustar jugar ...** to mean 'I like playing ...' but 'I play' is <u>jue</u>go ...

◎ **Escucha y escribe ✓ en la columna correcta.** Listen and write a ✓ in the correct column.

	a ♪♪♪	b 📖	c 🏃	d 🎥	e 🏍	f 👥
1						
2						
3						
4						
5						

! R E M E M B E R
Listening to Spanish when revising is not only useful for testing yourself or practising your exam technique. It can also help you learn, or re-learn, different ways of expressing things. Try to focus sometimes on <u>how</u> people say things, as well as <u>what</u> they say.

Did you notice that the second person said: **Oigo música** (I listen to music) and the fourth said: **Me gusta oír música** (I like listening to music)? Remember that you can use **me gusta** with an infinitive (the part of the verb ending in **'ar'**, **'er'** or **'ir'**) to mean 'I like ...': **Me gusta bailar** (I like dancing). To say what you *usually* do, you need to use the present tense of the verb: take off the **'ar'**, **'er'** or **'ir'** ending and add an **'o'**: bail<u>o</u> (<u>I</u> dance).

(?) Can you work out the Spanish for the following?

1 *me gusta escuchar música*   I like listening to music
2 .... *música*   I listen to music
3 *me gusta leer libros*   I like reading books
4 .... *libros*   I read books

Some verbs don't follow this pattern. Listen to the next three people (6, 7, and 8) on the same clip as before, and try to fill in the missing infinitive forms in the sentences below.

◎ **Escucha y completa las frases.** Listen and complete the sentences.

(Sport)   *Me gusta (6) .... deporte. Hago deporte.*
(Going out)   *Me gusta (7) .... con amigos. Salgo con amigos.*
(Cinema)   *Me gusta (8) .... al cine. Voy al cine.*

Going out

◎ When arranging to go out, times are frequently mentioned. Sometimes these might be given on tape or written down using the 24-hour clock. Make sure you understand how it works.

❓ What times are these in English and Spanish according to the 12-hour clock (i.e. half past twelve, four o'clock etc.): 13.00, 15.30, 20.15, 23.50?

There are always important questions to be asked when arranging to meet. Listen to the clip where Manuel telephones Enma to ask her out, and see if you can find the Spanish equivalents to the English phrases below.

31

❗ **REMEMBER** You'll learn faster if you have some fun in the process. Once you've seen a clip a few times, turn the sound down or off and then watch again – how much of the dialogue can you remember or lip-read?

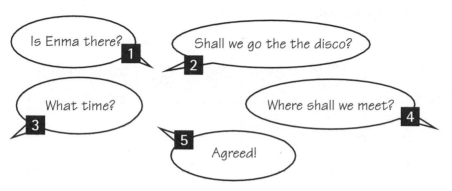

Is Enma there? **1**

Shall we go the the disco? **2**

What time? **3**

Where shall we meet? **4**

5 Agreed!

ⓗ You might be asked questions in English to test your understanding further. Watch the clip in which Vanesa and Ramón buy tickets for the cinema. Listen as often as you want – don't give up too easily.

1. *How many tickets does Vanesa ask for?*
2. *What did Ramón think of the film?*
3. *How is Ramón feeling?*
4. *What does he say he's going to do?*
5. *What suggestion does Vanesa make?*

❗ **REMEMBER** Don't worry if there's a picture or symbol left over in this type of activity – this is deliberate. Sometimes the instruction will tell you this: **sobra uno/a** (there's one extra).

Now try the exam-type practice activity below: the instruction is given only in Spanish. Find the clip in which Enma talks about her free time and which begins: **¿Qué te gusta hacer en tu tiempo libre?**

Practice activity

Escucha a Enma. Escribe las letras en las casillas apropiadas. ¡Atención – sobra una!

1. En mi tiempo libre ... ☐ ☐ ☐

2. Los fines de semana ... ☐ ☐

[a] [b] [c]

[d] [e] [f]

Speaking

Personal details

In the speaking exam, your teacher or examiner will almost certainly ask you for a few personal details, such as your name, age and birthday. It will give you confidence if you're well-prepared for these questions, so work your way carefully through this page.

Start with the Spanish alphabet. It's got one letter which the British alphabet doesn't have – can you remember what it is? In the list below, the words in brackets show you how to pronounce the letters in Spanish.

a *(ah)*	**j** *(hotta)*	**r** *(erray)*
b *(bay)*	**k** *(ka)*	**s** *(essay)*
c *(thay)*	**l** *(elay)*	**t** *(tay)*
d *(day)*	**m** *(emay)*	**u** *(oo)*
e *(ay)*	**n** *(enay)*	**v** *(oovay)*
f *(effay)*	**ñ** *(enyay)*	**w** *(oovay doblay)*
g *(hay)*	**o** *(oh)*	**x** *(aykees)*
h *(atch-ay)*	**p** *(pay)*	**y** *(ee gree ay ga)*
i *(ee)*	**q** *(coo)*	**z** *(thay ta)*

In the exam, you might be asked to spell your first name: **¿Cómo se escribe tu nombre?** or your surname: **¿Cómo se escribe tu apellido?**

◎ Practise the Spanish alphabet by spelling your name and the names of the members of your family.

In this next activity you can use the sports club register to make up more conversations just by changing the parts of the replies which are underlined. Read the sample conversation through first.

◎ Make up some interviews using the sports club register.

– *¿Cómo te llamas?*
+ *Me llamo <u>Marta.</u>*
– *¿Cuál es tu apellido?*
+ *Es <u>Duarte</u>.*
– *¿Cómo se escribe?*
+ *<u>D-U-A-R-T-E.</u>*
– *¿Cuántos años tienes?*
+ *Tengo <u>quince</u> años.*
– *¿Cuándo es tu cumpleaños?*
+ *Es el <u>uno de febrero</u>.*

CLUB DE DEPORTES			
	Apellido	Nombre	Edad	Cumpleaños
1	Duarte	Marta	15	1.2
2	Elizalde	Curro	14	29.8
3	Gallego	Javier	17	15.4
4	Moreno	Zohora	13	20.7
5	Tejero	Nuria	16	3.11

❗ REMEMBER It's very important that you learn how to pronounce the letters of the Spanish alphabet. You need to know how to spell names or write them down when someone else spells them.

❗ REMEMBER Every moment of practice helps! While you're waiting outside a classroom or in the lunch queue, try spelling the names of some of your classmates in Spanish for your friend(s) to work out.

Explaining what you're like

📺 You need to be able to respond to questions about what you look like: **¿Cómo es tu físico?** and what your personality is like: **De carácter, ¿cómo eres?**

❓ Use a dictionary to look up any of the words below you don't know.

(Height)	**Soy**	alto(a)/bajo(a)/de talla media.
(Shape)		delgado(a)/fuerte/gordito(a).
(Hair colour)	**Tengo el pelo**	marrón/rubio/negro.
(Hair length)		corto/largo/hasta el hombro.
(Hair texture)		rizado/liso/ondulado.
(Eyes)	**Tengo los ojos**	marrones/verdes/grises/azules.
	Llevo	gafas/lentillas.
(Personality)	**Soy**	simpático(a)/callado(a)/extrovertido(a).
		pesimista/optimista/hablador(a).
		alegre/amable/generoso(a).

An adjective which ends in **'o'** in the masculine form, will end in **'a'** in the feminine form. Use the words above to help you with this next activity.

◎ **Completa las palabras.** Complete the endings on Federico and Ana's descriptions.

¡Hola! Me llamo Federico. Soy bastante baj_ y fuert_. Tengo el pelo corto, rizado y marrón. De carácter, soy simpátic_ y alegr_.

¡Buenos días! Soy Ana. Soy alt_ y muy delgad_. Tengo los ojos verdes y el pelo rubio, largo y liso. De carácter, soy optimista y hablador_.

❓ Now talk about yourself – your height, shape, hair, eyes and personality. The words above and Federico and Ana's descriptions will help you.

You might also have to describe a member of your family or a friend. So have a look at these seven sentences from Alejandro's letter and do the activity.

◎ **¿Son las frases para Alejandro o para su hermano?** Is Alejandro describing himself or his brother?

1 Me llamo Alejandro y tengo dieciséis años.
2 Es alto y bastante delgado.
3 Mi cumpleaños es el treinta de octubre.
4 Soy simpático, pero un poco tímido.
5 Se llama Pepe y es mayor que yo.
6 Tengo el pelo liso, corto y negro.
7 Tiene los ojos marrones y lleva gafas.

Did you notice that when talking about someone else, you need to use **tiene** (he/she has), **es** (he/she is) and **lleva** (he/she wears)?

❓ Try to describe a member of your family or a friend, using **tiene**, **es** and **lleva** along with any words you need from above. Use **su** for his/her.

! REMEMBER
When you look up a Spanish word in the dictionary, check its spelling carefully before you start. If you can't find a word, it might be because you're not looking it up correctly.

! REMEMBER
Your description will be more interesting if you add extra words like **bastante** (quite, fairly), **muy** (very), **algo** (rather), or **un poco** (a little, a bit).

Speaking

Making arrangements

When arranging to go out, you'll need to give a time. To pinpoint a day of the week, use **el**: **¿Quieres salir el viernes?** (Do you want to go out on Friday?) To give a specific time of day, use **de**: **¿Nos vemos a las diez de la noche?** (Shall we meet at 10p.m?) To refer to a general time of day, use **por**: **Te llamo por la tarde, ¿vale?** (I'll ring you in the afternoon, OK?)

Lee la conversación y rellena los huecos con 'el', 'por' o 'de'. Read the conversation and fill the gaps with **el, por** or **de.**

JAVI: ¡Oiga, Marifé! Soy Javi. ¿Quieres ir al cine conmigo ..(1).. viernes?

MARIFÉ: Lo siento, no puedo. Tengo que ir al centro con Alicia a las tres ..(2).. la tarde.

JAVI: Vamos todos a la discoteca el sábado ..(3).. la noche – ¿quieres venir?

MARIFÉ: Lo siento. Tengo que cuidar a mi hermano. ¿Estás libre ..(4).. domingo?

JAVI: ..(5).. la tarde solamente.

MARIFÉ: No sé. Te llamo mañana ..(6).. la mañana, ¿vale?

Now try to make up another conversation with these details.

Javi invites Marifé to the bowling alley, but she can't go because she's going to the pool. Javi then suggests the ice-rink but Marifé has to look after her sister. Javi is only free on Sunday night, so Marifé promises to ring him in the afternoon.

If you're arranging where to meet, you'll need to ask: **¿Dónde nos vemos?** (Where shall we meet?) and **¿A qué hora nos vemos?** (When shall we meet?). You'll also need to describe where to meet.

Empareja las palabras españolas con las palabras inglesas. Match the Spanish words to their English meaning.

1 entre	a in front (of)
2 enfrente (de)	b behind
3 detrás (de)	c opposite
4 al lado (de)	d between
5 delante (de)	e beside/next to

Use the cues in the box to make up some more conversations.

– ¿Dónde nos vemos?
+ ¿Nos vemos <u>detrás del mercado</u>?
– Vale. ¿A qué hora nos vemos?
+ ¿A <u>las ocho y media</u>?
– Muy bien. ¡Hasta luego!
+ ¡Adiós!

1 opposite the park (5.15)
2 in front of the café (11.00)
3 next to the cinema (9.00)
4 behind the church (12.45)

! REMEMBER Other useful time phrases are **esta mañana** (this morning), **esta tarde** (this afternoon/evening) and **esta noche** (tonight).

! REMEMBER When **de** is followed by **el**, they join together to form **del.**

Talking about time, frequency and seasons

You can add more detail to your conversation or presentation by explaining *when* you do activities. You might go to a club at lunchtime (**en la hora de comer**) or after school (**después de las clases**), but it will useful to know a wider range of time phrases.

◎ Read the list below – can you work how to say the expressions on the right in Spanish? Change the underlined words.

1 en *primavera* (in spring)	**in summer, in autumn, in winter?**
2 en *enero* (in January)	**in September?**
3 una vez por *semana* (once a week)	**once a month?**
4 *dos* veces por semana (twice a week)	**three times a week?**
5 los *viernes* por la noche (on Friday nights)	**on Monday nights?**
6 los *jueves/domingos* (on Thursdays/Sundays)	**on Tuesdays/Saturdays?**
7 el *doce de mayo* (on 12th May)	**on 16th June?**

◎ **Practica la conversación siguiente con tu pareja.** Practise the conversation below with a friend.

– ¿Qué te gusta hacer en tu tiempo libre?
+ ..(1).. me gusta jugar al baloncesto.
  Juego al fútbol y practico la natación ..(2)..
– ¿Eres miembro de algún club?
+ Soy miembro del club de ordenadores.
  Nos reunimos ..(3)..
– ¿Tocas algún instrumento?
+ El martes ..(4).. tengo clase de guitarra.
– ¿Qué haces el fin de semana?
+ ..(5).. salgo con mis amigos a la discoteca.
  Y hago mis deberes ..(6)..

1 in winter
2 in July and August
3 twice a week
4 after school
5 on Friday nights
6 on Sundays

◎ **Contesta a las preguntas.** Answer the questions from the conversation above for yourself. Make sure you use appropriate expressions of time.

! REMEMBER Keep revising the months of the year and days of the week – try starting at December or Sunday and working backwards for a change!

! REMEMBER You are not allowed to 'read' your presentation in the exam: get used to writing a few 'prompt' words on small cards to help you remember what you want to say.

Practice activity

You might have to give a presentation as part of your speaking exam, and talking about your free time is a popular theme. You can talk about:

– the sports and activities you do
– when you do them
– what you do or don't like doing and why
– which clubs you're a member of
– what you do at the weekend.

Try to give a very short presentation: prepare a few sentences on one of the suggestions on the left and practise it in front of the mirror. Then try the other suggestions. Try and build up to speak for two or three minutes. 'Prompt' cards like these might help you:

baloncesto – aburrido

fútbol/atletismo (verano)

Leisure

You already know how important it is to know the days of the week, the months and times of day. Have you learnt them? Try the following activity to find out.

◎ **Contesta a las preguntas en inglés.** Answer the questions in English.

1 *Who can go to the club? (1)*
2 *On which days does it meet? (2)*
3 *Name two activities you can do there. (2)*
4 *During which months is it open until 8p.m? (2)*

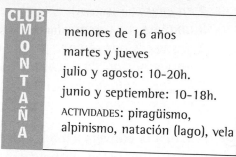

CLUB MONTAÑA

menores de 16 años
martes y jueves
julio y agosto: 10-20h.
junio y septiembre: 10-18h.
ACTIVIDADES: piragüismo, alpinismo, natación (lago), vela

In Spanish, as in English, there's often more than one way of saying the same thing. For example, **hacer footing** and **hacer jogging** mean 'to go jogging'.

◎ Can you join up the expressions below which mean the same thing?

1 *hacer footing*
2 *salir en pandilla*
3 *montar a caballo*
4 *pescar*
5 *bailar*
6 *ir al cine*
7 *hacer natación*

a *ir de pesca*
b *hacer equitación*
c *nadar*
d *ver una película*
e *salir con amigos*
f *hacer jogging*
g *ir a la discoteca*

Now read the short paragraph below and do the activity.

◎ **Lee la carta. ¿Verdad o mentira?** Read the letter. True or false?

Los sábados o los domingos por la mañana, practico la natación con mi familia - hay una piscina en el polideportivo cerca de casa. Entre semana, hago footing: soy miembro de un club. Cuando hace mal tiempo y no puedo salir, veo la tele o leo - me encanta la lectura. Los viernes por la tarde, salgo con mis amigos y vamos a la discoteca o al cine. *NURIA*

	verdad	mentira
1 *El fin de semana, a Nuria le gusta nadar.*	☐	☐
2 *El centro de deportes está lejos.*	☐	☐
3 *Nuria juega al fútbol.*	☐	☐
4 *Le gusta mucho leer.*	☐	☐
5 *No le interesa mucho bailar.*	☐	☐
6 *Le gustan las películas.*	☐	☐

Invitations

Matching pictures or symbols to pieces of text is a popular type of task in the exam. When the texts are a little longer, you'll have to hunt around more for the answer. You might find it useful to look at the pictures or symbols first and work out what each one is about. For example, if you see a picture of a group of young people, you might think of the Spanish words **grupo** (group), **jóvenes** (young), **amigos** (friends) or **salir** (to go out). Then 'skim read' the texts by quickly running your eye down each one to see where any of those words or similar words appear. Then read the texts again, more closely this time, and see which one matches the picture best. You can then move on to the next picture, and so on. Try that technique with this next activity.

R E M E M B E R
You can write your answers in pencil on the exam paper until you've finished the task. Once you think you've got all the answers right, fill them in with a pen or a biro.

◉ **Empareja las invitaciones con los símbolos.** Match the invitations to the symbols.

| A3 | | | | | |

A Cristina, gracias por la invitación a salir contigo y tus amigos a la feria. Lo siento, pero no puedo - las entradas cuestan demasiado. Pero te llamaré el sábado, ¿vale? Tere.

B ¡Hola, Juana! No puedo salir contigo esta noche porque voy a visitar a mis abuelos. Pero ¿quieres ir a la pista de hielo mañana? Te llamo. Irene.

C Sofía, voy al nuevo centro comercial esta tarde. ¿Te gustaría venir? Merche.

D TOMÁS: NO QUIERO SALIR AL CONCIERTO ESTA TARDE. NO ME SIENTO MUY BIEN. QUIERO QUEDARME EN CASA. LLÁMAME. PALOMA

E Miguel - gracias por tu invitación al partido de baloncesto el sábado, pero no puedo venir. Tengo que cuidar a mi hermano menor desde las diez de la mañana hasta las ocho de la tarde. ¡Otro día será! Carlos.

F Victor - lo siento mucho, pero no puedo venir a merendar mañana. Tengo muchos deberes. ¿Nos vemos el jueves? Marina.

 1  3 4   5 6 7

Sometimes you might have to match pieces of text to sentences or definitions. In the next activity, you have to pair up each of the teenagers A–F above with the most appropriate sentence 1–6 below. You need to do some detective work: which is the most likely person, given what you know about them? For example, number 1 says: 'I have to go shopping' – well, this might be true for almost any of the young people above, but only one of them mentions the kind of place you might go to for shopping (C mentions **el centro comercial**). Can you pair up the rest?

◉ **Para cada frase 1–6, elige la persona más adecuada A–F.** For each sentence 1–6, choose the most appropriate person above A–F.

1 *Tengo que ir de compras.* C

2 *Tengo que estudiar.*

3 *No tengo suficiente dinero.*

4 *No tengo ganas de salir.*

5 *No tengo tiempo.*

6 *Tengo que visitar a mis parientes.*

R E M E M B E R
Tengo means 'I have' and **tengo que** means 'I have to'.

Reading

Opinions

You might read about people's opinions on sports and hobbies in the exam and you could come across words such as **divertido** (fun), **aburrido** (boring), **competitivo** (competitive), **peligroso** (dangerous), **relajante** (relaxing), **emocionante** (exciting), **caro** (expensive) and **barato** (cheap). Sometimes you might get a task where you have to choose words to fill gaps in a text. In this type of activity it's very important to read for meaning and to read carefully what comes before and after the gap.

(?) Would you complete this sentence with **divertido** or **aburrido**?

Dani: Me gusta mucho tocar la guitarra, porque es ...

It should be **divertido** (fun) because Dani says he *likes* playing the guitar so it wouldn't make sense with **aburrido**. Now try these sentences.

◎ **Subraya la palabra correcta.** Underline the correct word.

1 *No me gusta jugar al rugby –* es **aburrido/emocionante**.
2 *Lo malo del alpinismo es que es* **peligroso/divertido**.
3 *La equitación es* **cara/barata** *y no tengo mucho dinero*.
4 *Odio el fútbol porque es* **relajante/competitivo**.

! REMEMBER Don't worry if you can't understand all the words on the page. Just try to pick out the key words.

Sometimes the word directly before the choice of words can give you a clue. If it's singular (**un, una, el, la, mi**) or plural (**unos, unas, los, las, mis**) this tells you whether you need to choose the singular or the plural word.

(?) What would you underline in this sentence?

Mis **padre/padres** *son simpáticos*.

The answer is **padres** because **mis** is a plural word. Now try these activities.

◎ **Subraya la palabra correcta.** Underline the correct word.

1 *Mi* **hermana/hermanas** *es mayor que yo*.
2 *No me gustan los* **fútbol/deportes**. *Prefiero algo más relajante*.
3 *Tengo un* **amigo/amigos** *especial, que se llama Eduardo*.
4 *Las* **chica/chicas** *de mi clase son simpáticas*.

◎ **Escribe el número correcto en cada casilla.** Write the correct number in each box.

1 madre
2 natación
3 agosto
4 nadar
5 divertidos
6 padres
7 llamo
8 tiempo
9 aburrida

ME PRESENTO: me [7] Quino y vivo aquí en San Sebastián con mis [ ] y mi hermana Julia. ¡Qué bien que vienes aquí para pasar quince días con nosotros en [ ]! ¿Qué te gusta hacer en tu [ ] libre? Cuando hace calor, prefiero [ ] en el mar – ¡la piscina es muy [ ]! A mí, me gustan los deportes de equipo, porque son muy [ ]. Cada noche, juego al voleibol o al fútbol con mis amigos en el parque.

Pocket money

A good vocabulary is essential for the exam. You might be allowed to use a dictionary, but if you have to look up every word, you'll never finish in time. See how fast you can group the items in this activity – with or without the help of a dictionary.

◎ **Pon los números en la casilla correcta.** Put the numbers in the correct box.

Cosas para comer (things to eat)
5

Ropa (clothes)

Lugares de diversión (leisure places)

Música (music)

Cosas para leer (things to read)

1 bolera
2 camiseta
3 caramelos
4 cassettes
5 churros
6 cintas
7 club juvenil
8 discos compactos
9 galletas
10 jersey
11 libros
12 pantalón
13 polideportivo
14 revistas
15 tebeos

> **! REMEMBER**
> In very up-to-date dictionaries, words which begin with 'ch' in Spanish will be found in the 'C' section, as in English. However if your dictionary is slightly older, you may find them in a separate section of their own, after the 'C' section.

Practice activity

This practice activity brings together all the things you've been revising on the last few pages. Remember to read for meaning and don't just look for the same words in the article as in the questions.

◎ **Escribe el nombre de la persona más apropiada.**
Ejemplo: ¿Quién es miembro de una familia numerosa? – Sabrina

1 ¿Quién es deportista?

....

2 ¿Quién tiene que trabajar el fin de semana? ....

3 ¿Quién gasta todo su dinero?

....

4 ¿Quién tiene que estudiar mucho?

....

5 ¿Quién no recibe dinero de sus padres? ....

6 ¿Quién trabaja entre semana?

....

¿RECIBES DINERO? ¿CUÁNTO? ¿CUÁNDO?

1 Mi madrastra es enfermera, y tiene que trabajar mucho. ¡Yo también! Cuido a mis hermanas (de dos y cinco años) los sábados y los domingos. El dinero que gano lo uso para pagarme cursos de piragüismo, o ala delta, en la montaña durante las vacaciones. ISABEL

2 No me dan mucho dinero mis padres porque somos seis hermanas en total. Y no trabajo fuera de casa: tengo exámenes en junio y no tengo tiempo para salir. Cada noche tengo un montón de deberes - ¡demasiados! SABRINA.

3 Yo gano dinero trabajando en el garaje de un amigo de mi padre, de lunes a viernes. Empiezo a las seis y termino a las diez. Me gusta ganar mi propio dinero - no quiero depender de mis padres. PAUL

4 Mis padres me dan diez mil pesetas al mes - parece mucho, pero tengo que pagar todo: la ropa, los libros, las diversiones, las entradas, las cosas personales - aún los viajes en autobús para ir al instituto. A finales del mes, ¡no tengo ni un duro! ENRIQUE.

Sports and hobbies

(TV) Don't be put off by having to write Spanish in the exam – sometimes you'll just have to write single words or short sentences. Some sports and hobbies in Spanish are identical to English (**el rugby**) and some sound similar but they are spelled slightly differently (**el fútbol**).

◎ **Completa las palabras correctamente.** Complete the words correctly.

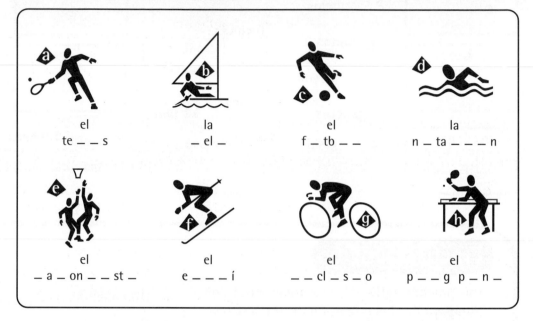

el
te _ _ s

la
_ el _

el
f _ tb _ _

la
n _ ta _ _ _ n

el
_ a _ on _ _ st _

el
e _ _ _ í

el
_ _ cl _ s _ o

el
p _ _ g p _ n _

> **!** R E M E M B E R
> The only double letters in Spanish words are '**rr**' and '**ll**' unless they're in a 'borrowed word' like **el footing** or **el jogging.** There is only one '**n**' in **el te<u>n</u>is**!

When you're writing about the sports you play or do, you need to decide whether to use **juego** (I play) or **practico** (I do/I go/I practise). The general rule below will help:

> **juego**
> *Use with ball sports, where you would say 'I play ...' in English:*
> **Juego al hockey**
> *(I play hockey).*

> **practico**
> *Use where you would say 'I do/I go ...' in English:*
> **Practico la natación**
> *(I go swimming).*

> **!** R E M E M B E R
> After **juego** you need to use **al** with a masculine (**el**) activity: **el golf -> juego al golf.** If you want to say you play cards, write **juego a las cartas.**

◎ Look again at the pictures of the sports activities a–h above. Try writing a full sentence for each picture this time, using either **juego (al ...)** or **practico (el .../la ...).**

You can also use **hago** instead of **practico**, but you leave out the **el** or **a**: **practico el atletismo -> hago atletismo.**

◎ Can you make a list of sports or hobbies, using **hago**?

Likes and dislikes

📺 When explaining which sports you like or dislike, you need to use an infinitive (such as **jugar, practicar** and **hacer**) after **(no) me gusta**.

◎ **Escribe frases para Merche, Felipe, Catalina, Raúl y Javier.** Write sentences for Merche, Felipe, Catalina, Raúl and Javier.

Ejemplo:
Merche: Me gusta jugar al rugby, pero no me gusta practicar la natación.

	❤❤	✖✖
MERCHE	el rugby	la natación
FELIPE	el footing	el golf
CATALINA	el alpinismo	el voleibol
RAÚL	el piragüismo	el rugby
JAVIER	el hockey	la equitación

There are lots of ways of saying you like or don't like an activity. As well as **me gusta** (I like) you can expand your range by using **me encanta** (I love), **me interesa** (I'm interested in), **odio/detesto** (I hate) and **no aguanto** (I can't stand).

❓ Try and answer each of these questions using a different expression for liking or disliking.

¿Te gusta jugar al fútbol?

¿Qué opinas de la natación?

¿Te gusta practicar la gimnasia?

¿Qué deportes te gusta hacer en invierno?

¿Qué actividades deportivas haces en verano?

It's important to give your reasons for liking or disliking an activity. You could choose from the following:

Es .... – It's ...

divertido/a – fun	*aburrido/a* – boring
emocionante – exciting	*peligroso/a* – dangerous
caro/a – expensive	*barato/a* – cheap

un deporte individual – an individual sport
un deporte de equipo – a team sport

❓ Try and complete the sentences below with a sporting activity.

Ejemplo: Me gusta hacer alpinismo porque es divertido.

Me gusta .... porque es divertido.
Me gusta bastante .... – no está mal.
No me gusta mucho .... porque no es muy interesante.
Odio ....: ¡es súper aburrido!

Personal Life

REMEMBER
You can make your writing more interesting by using variations of **me gusta**, such as: **me gusta bastante** (I quite like), **me gusta mucho** (I really like), **no me gusta nada** (I don't like ... at all).

REMEMBER
When you're describing an activity, the adjective, such as **divertido/a**, has to end in 'o' for a masculine (**el**) activity: <u>el</u> **fútbol es divertid<u>o</u>**. The adjective has to end in 'a' if the activity is feminine (**la**): <u>la</u> **natación es divertid<u>a</u>**.

REMEMBER
When you want to ask 'why' use the two words **¿por qué?** To say 'because', use **porque**.

Writing

Writing about yourself and your family

In the writing exam you might have to fill in an ID form in Spanish, or a form for an exchange with a Spanish-speaking student. You'll need to be able to give details about yourself and your family – but first of all you need to understand the headings on the form. Read the one below carefully and look up any words you don't know in the dictionary. Then think about the information you're going to need and make sure you put the details in the correct sections.

◎ **Rellena la ficha con tus detalles personales.** Fill in the form with your personal details.

1 Nombre y apellido: _____

2 Nacionalidad: _____

3 Fecha de nacimiento: _____ Lugar de nacimiento: _____

4 Miembros de la familia: _____

5 Animales: _____

6 Pelo: _____ Ojos: _____

Practice activity

You don't just have to write in the writing exam – you'll need to read Spanish too. You might get a letter to reply to with specific information.

(?) Which of the following topics do you have to reply to in this letter? Choose from: your age, birthday, nationality, character, pets, free time, family and what you look like.

The answer is all of them! Iñigo asks you four questions, which are easy to spot as they have question marks around them. Did you spot the two 'hidden' questions? One begins with **descríbeme** (describe) and the other **cuéntame** (tell me).

h **Escribe una carta a Iñigo. Contesta a sus preguntas.**

¡Hola!

Me llamo Iñigo y vivo en Colombia, en América Latina. Tengo diecisiete años, y mi cumpleaños es el once de mayo. ¿Cuándo es tu cumpleaños? ¿Cuántos años tienes?

En mi familia, somos cuatro: mi padre, mi madre, mi hermana Clara y yo. Clara tiene quince años – es amable y alegre en general, pero muy curiosa. ¡Me irrita mucho! En tu próxima carta, descríbeme tu familia.

Soy bastante alto y un poco fuerte, con el pelo negro y rizado y los ojos morenos. Mi hermana dice que soy antipático, ¡pero no es verdad! ¿Y tú, cómo eres de carácter? ¿Y cómo es tu físico? Mándame una foto. Tenemos dos animales – una gata (Mimi) y un perro (Pepe). ¿Tú tienes animales en casa?

En mi tiempo libre, me encanta jugar al baloncesto. ¡Es súper divertido! Pero no aguanto hacer vela, porque es muy aburrida. Cuéntame lo que te gusta hacer (¡o no!) en tu tiempo libre.

Iñigo

GrammarZONE

The Spanish words for 'I', 'you', 'he', 'she' etc. are listed below. You probably remember that there are four words for 'you', depending on whether you're talking to one person or to more than one person, and whether you know them well (a familiar relationship) or not very well (a more formal relationship).

(?) Can you match the Spanish words to their English meaning? Don't forget to check your answers at the back!

yo	*you (one person, formal)*
tú	*she*
él	*you (more than one person, formal)*
ella	*we*
usted	*they (female)*
nosotros	*you (one person, familiar)*
vosotros	*I*
ellos	*he*
ellas	*they (male)*
ustedes	*you (more than one person, familiar)*

These words are called 'subject pronouns'. In English, we need to use them to explain who we're talking about: 'I am shy' but 'He is sociable – we are very different'. You don't always need to use these words in Spanish, because the way the verb changes also tells you this: **soy** means 'I am' and **somos** means 'we are'.

The following three verbs are used a lot in Spanish – let's look at the pattern:

	ser *(to be)*	**tener** *(to have)*	**ir** *(to go)*
yo	*soy*	*tengo*	*voy*
tú	*eres*	*tienes*	*vas*
él, ella, usted	*es*	*tiene*	*va*
nosotros	*somos*	*tenemos*	*vamos*
vosotros	*sóis*	*tenéis*	*vais*
ellos, ellas, ustedes	*son*	*tienen*	*van*

If you've mentioned someone's name, or you're talking about someone else and you don't know which part of the verb to use, remember the following:

- *talking about one person (e.g. Jake, Kate)? Think 'he/she'* – **él/ella**.
- *talking about more than one person (e.g. Mum and Dad)? Think 'they'* – **ellos/ellas**.
- *talking about you and someone else (e.g. my friend and I)? Think 'we'* – **nosotros**.

◎ Can you alter the verbs in brackets below so that the endings are correct?

*Yo (**1 ser**) Clara, y (**2 tener**) dieciséis años. Mis dos hermanos, Juanjo y Felipe, (**3 ser**) altos y delgados como mi padre. Él (**4 tener**) cuarenta y cinco años y (**5 ser**) simpático. Mi madre y yo (**6 ser**) más bajas, pero ella (**7 tener**) el pelo y los ojos morenos y yo (**8 ser**) rubia. Somos muy amigas. El sábado por la mañana, mi madre (**9 ir**) a la gimnasia con mi padre pero después, ella y yo (**10 ir**) de compras en el centro – ¡lo pasamos bomba! ¿Y vosotros – cómo (**11 ser**) en vuestra familia?*

The World Around Us

This section is about

- Home town and area

- Finding the way

- Weather

- Shopping

This section is all about where you live and what you think of it, giving and getting directions, understanding information about the weather and going shopping.

Home town and area

Spanish towns and villages vary greatly in their style. In the north, there are lots of fishing villages built of local stone; in the central plains, there are small towns built along the contours of the hills; and in the south, whitewashed towns with narrow, flower-bedecked streets are to be found. Every town or village has a main square (**la plaza mayor**) and café, where people catch up on the gossip and watch the world go by. Many towns have an old quarter (**el barrio antiguo**), often centred around a church or cathedral, and a more modern area (**la zona nueva**) around it stretching out into the suburbs.

Finding the way

When you arrive in a Spanish town, the first place to head for is the tourist office (**la oficina de información y turismo**), where you can get a town plan (**un plano**) and a brochure (**un folleto turístico**). Don't be afraid to ask for directions – and if you need the speaker to speak more slowly, just ask: **¿Puede hablar más despacio, por favor?**

Weather

Spain is not all beaches and sunshine. The north and west of Spain has a mild, damp climate and is known as **España Verde** (Green Spain) because of its high rainfall. The central area of Spain, including the capital Madrid, is over 600 metres above sea-level – in summer, this high plain (**meseta**) is very dry and hot and in winter it has biting winds and snowfall. The southern parts of Spain and the Balearic Islands have a Mediterranean climate: mild winters and hot, sunny summers. The temperatures inland in the south can reach over 40ºC and the town of Ecija is called 'the frying pan of Spain' (**la sartén de España**).

Shopping

Spanish shopping times are different from those in Britain. Many smaller shops (**tiendas**) still maintain the traditional pattern of opening hours: 9–1 and 5–8 with a long lunch break in the middle. Bigger stores (**los grandes almacenes**) are open all day without a break (**sin interrupción**) from 9a.m. to 9p.m. The local market (**el mercado**) is still a popular place to shop, although it tends to close by lunchtime. City dwellers tend to do their daily shopping for fruit, vegetables, meat and fish in their local area, although they might go to a hypermarket (**el hipermercado**) at the weekend. So let's get started – **¡vámonos!**

◉ These phrases will be really useful for your exam, so see if you can try and learn them!

Home town and area

¿Dónde vives? Where do you live?

Vivo ... en una ciudad (grande)/un pueblo.
    I live ... in a (big) town/village.

¿Qué hay para los turistas/los jóvenes?
    What is there for tourists/young people?

*Hay una iglesia, un castillo, una plaza de
    toros, un polideportivo, un cine, una
    pista de hielo.*   There's a church,
    castle, bull-ring, sports centre, cinema,
    ice-rink.

¿Cómo es? What's it like?

*Es aburrido/divertido, contaminado/limpio,
    bonito/feo.*   It's boring/fun,
    polluted/clean, pretty/ugly.

¿Te gusta vivir allí? Do you like living there?

Lo bueno/lo malo es que ...
    The good/bad thing is that ...

(No) hay mucho para los jóvenes.
    There is(n't) a lot for young people.

Finding the way

Por favor, ¿hay (un/una ...) por aquí?
    Excuse me, is there (a ...) near here?

¿Dónde está/están ...?   Where is/are ...?

¿Para ir al/a la/a los/a las ...?
    How do you get to the ...?

Está/están en la calle .../en la avenida ...
    It's/they are in ... Street/... Avenue.

detrás de/delante de/enfrente de/entre ...
    behind/in front of/opposite/between ...

al lado de/cerca de/lejos de ...
    beside/near/far from ...

*A unos (cinco) minutos/kilómetros en
    coche/andando.*   About (five)
    minutes/kilometres away by car/on foot.

Weather

¿Qué tiempo hace en ...?   What's the
    weather like in ...?

en primavera/verano/otoño/invierno
    in spring/summer/autumn/winter

Hace buen tiempo/hace bueno.
    The weather is good.

Hace mal tiempo/hace malo.
    The weather is bad.

Hace frío/calor/viento/sol.
    It's cold/hot/windy/sunny.

Hay neblina/niebla/tormenta.
    It's misty/foggy/stormy.

Llueve/está lloviendo.   It rains/it is raining.

Hay nieve/está nevando.
    There's snow/it is snowing.

Está nublado, está despejado.
    It's cloudy, the sky is clear.

Shopping

¿Qué desea?   What would you like?

Quiero/quisiera ...   I want/I'd like ...

¿Algo más? ¿Es todo?   Anything else? Is that
    all?

No, nada mas.   No, nothing else.

¿Cuánto es/cuesta?   How much is it/does it
    cost?

Son ... pesetas.   It's ... pesetas.

¿Tiene cambio?   Have you got change?

Sólo tengo un billete de (cinco mil) pesetas.
    I've only got a (5000) peseta note.

¿Cómo quiere pagar?   How do you want to
    pay?

En metálico/efectivo. Con tarjeta de crédito.
    By cash. With a credit card.

The World Around Us

Your home town

Numbers always seem to find their way into every topic! When listening to information about where people live, you might have to note the number of inhabitants (**habitantes**), the proportion of the population (**población**) that lives in the capital, the height (**altura**) of the town above sea-level or the number of tourists who visit the place every year.

Find the clip which describes Mexico City and do the following activity.

◎ **Escucha y rellena los huecos.** Listen and fill in the gaps with the correct number.

1 Hoy en día, hay más de .... millones de habitantes.	**2000**
2 En el año dos mil, habrá unos .... (milliones).	**¼**
3 México está situada a .... metros de altura.	**30**
4 Un .... de la población del país vive en la capital.	**900**
5 Casi la .... de la industria está aquí.	**19**
	½

What do you think about the place where you live, and why do you like it – or not? There are lots of possibilities – and one person's reason for liking a place may be someone else's reason for hating it. Perhaps it's quiet there (**tranquilo**) or everyone knows everyone else (**todo el mundo se conoce**) or there might be lots to do (**hay mucho que hacer**), or nothing to do (**no hay nada que hacer**).

Find the clip where some teenagers discuss the advantages of both village and town life. They are asked: **¿Qué prefieres, la ciudad o el pueblo?**

◎ **Escucha y escribe ✓ en las casillas correctas.** Listen and put a ✓ in the correct boxes.

Prefiero vivir en un pueblo porque ...

1 es más pequeño. ☐
2 es más tranquilo. ☐
3 todo el mundo se conoce. ☐
4 me gustan el campo y los animales. ☐
5 no hay mucha contaminación. ☐

Prefiero vivir en una ciudad porque ...

6 es más grande. ☐
7 es más interesante. ☐
8 hay más cosas que hacer. ☐
9 hay más tiendas. ☐
10 me gusta el ambiente. ☐

Out and about

The following section of listening is almost certainly longer than anything you will have in the exam, but it's excellent practice. Find the clip about Zujaira which begins: **Zujaira es un pueblo muy chiquito** and play it several times as you do the activity.

◎ **Empareja las dos partes de las frases. Sobra una parte.** Match the two halves of the sentences. There is one left over.

1 *Zujaira no es grande. Tiene...*	*a en la Vega.*
2 *Las casas tienen ...*	*b iglesia.*
3 *Todos los pueblos tienen ...*	*c una piscina.*
4 *En la fuente hay ...*	*d dos mil habitantes.*
5 *Muchos habitantes trabajan en ...*	*e todo el mundo se conoce.*
6 *Zujaira tiene una fábrica de ...*	*f aceitunas.*
7 *A los jóvenes, les gustaría tener ...*	*g agua de la sierra.*
8 *Les gusta el pueblo porque*	*h aceite de oliva.*
	i dos plantas.

1	2	3	4	5	6	7	8
d							

47

In the next activity you're going to hear directions – and that's a common exam activity. Before you start, check that you know the Spanish for 'straight on', 'left' and 'right'.

⟨?⟩ Now look at these maps. Do you know how to direct somebody to each of the places marked a–c on the maps?

The World Around Us

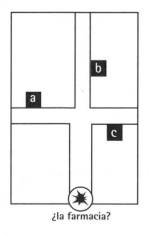

¿la farmacia?

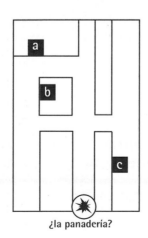

¿la panadería?

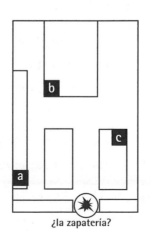

¿la zapatería?

Find the clip where Ana organises a treasure hunt in her local area.

◎ **Escucha las tres indicaciones y escoge la letra correcta.** Listen to the three sets of directions and choose the correct letter on each map.

ⓣ Listening

Shopping

If you go clothes shopping, you'll need to know about sizes and colours. The size might be given as a number (**talla 40**) or as large (**grande**), medium (**mediano**) or small (**pequeño**).

◎ Find the clip where Vanesa, Israel, Ramón and Sara go shopping, and play the tape with no sound. Look at the clothes they're wearing (not what they're buying) and complete these descriptions with a colour.

> **REMEMBER** Learn the words for shades of colour as well: **oscuro** (dark), **claro** (light), **vivo** (bright) and **azul marino** (navy).

Vanesa lleva un jersey ....

Israel lleva una chaqueta ....

Ramón lleva una camisa ....

Sara lleva una rebeca ....

azul marino	amarilla
beige	gris
negro	marrón
azul claro	rosa
roja	verde
blanca	naranja

If you get multiple-choice questions, like the ones below, you need to read them carefully first. Sometimes they're very similar, as in 1a, b and c, so it's important you don't confuse them and tick the wrong box. Your exam board may allow you a few moments to read through the paper before and after the test with a dictionary, but you won't be allowed to use one while the tape is playing. Read through the activity below and only look up the words you really do not know at all: give yourself one minute only.

◎ **Escucha y escribe ✓ en las casillas apropiadas.** Listen and put a ✓ in the appropriate boxes.

> **REMEMBER** If you change your mind after ticking a box and want to tick another one, then make sure you score out your first answer. If the examiner sees two ticks, you will get no marks!

1 Vanesa busca:
- ☐ *a una camisa mediana*
- ☐ *b una camiseta pequeña*
- ☐ *c una camisa grande.*

2 Israel quiere:
- ☐ *a una cazadora mediana*
- ☐ *b una cazadora pequeña*
- ☐ *c una camisa pequeña.*

3 Ramón quiere:
- ☐ *a unos pantalones beige*
- ☐ *b unos pantalones marrones*
- ☐ *c unos pantalones grises.*

4 Ramón necesita la talla:
- ☐ *a 21*
- ☐ *b 31*
- ☐ *c 30.*

5 Hay también chaquetas en:
- ☐ *a negro y naranja*
- ☐ *b blanco y marrón*
- ☐ *c naranja y blanco.*

6 Sara va a probarse:
- ☐ *a la naranja*
- ☐ *b la blanca*
- ☐ *c la roja.*

Practice activity

Paying for items inevitably involves numbers – sometimes large ones.

Check that you can say these prices.
Ejemplo: *a doscientas pesetas*

a 200 ptas.	*d 1.435 ptas.*
b 595 ptas.	*e 5.720 ptas.*
c 805 ptas.	*f 10.999 ptas.*

GrammarZONE

When you look up a Spanish verb in the dictionary, you'll notice that it has one of the following three endings: **–ar, –er, –ir**. This part of the verb is called an 'infinitive' and it means '<u>to</u> do something' For example, **escucha<u>r</u>** (<u>to</u> listen), **le<u>er</u>** (<u>to</u> read), **viv<u>ir</u>** (<u>to</u> live). The following expressions use infinitives after them in Spanish (although English sometimes uses '-ing').

Quiero <u>visitar</u> el castillo.	>	*I want to visit the castle.*
Voy a <u>ver</u> la catedral.	>	*I'm going to see the cathedral.*
No me gusta <u>vivir</u> aquí.	>	*I don't like living here.*

◉ Fill the gaps with the Spanish infinitive verb – you can use a dictionary if you need to.

1 Me gusta .... las tiendas pequeñas.	(to explore)
2 Voy a .... recuerdos para llevar a casa.	(to look for)
3 Quiero .... algo típico.	(to buy)
4 No quiero .... mucho.	(to spend)
5 Tengo que .... a Gran Bretaña mañana.	(to go back to)

In Spanish you don't always need the words for 'I', 'you' etc. because the ending of the verb gives you this information: **escuch<u>o</u>** means '<u>I</u> listen' and **vivi<u>mos</u>** means '<u>we</u> live'. Look at these patterns in the present tense:

	escuchar	leer	vivir
	(to listen)	(to read)	(to live)
yo	*escuch**o***	*le**o***	*viv**o***
tú	*escuch**as***	*le**es***	*viv**es***
él, ella, usted	*escuch**a***	*le**e***	*viv**e***
nosotros	*escuch**amos***	*le**emos***	*viv**imos***
vostros	*escuch**áis***	*le**éis***	*viv**ís***
ellos, ellas, ustedes	*escuch**an***	*le**en***	*viv**en***

Some verbs are slightly irregular in the **yo** form, but regular in all other parts:

conocer	to know (a person)	*conozco*	I know (a person)
dar	to give	*doy*	I give
hacer	to do, make	*hago*	I do, make
poner	to put, set, lay	*pongo*	I put, set, lay
saber	to know (a fact)	*sé*	I know (a fact)
salir	to go out	*salgo*	I go out
traer	to bring	*traigo*	I bring
ver	to see, watch	*veo*	I see, watch

◉ Change the verbs in brackets below so that the endings are correct.

Yo soy Clara, y (**1 vivir**) *.................................... en San Sebastián en el norte de España.*
En mi tiempo libre en invierno, (**2 escuchar**) *.................................... música y*
(**3 leer**) *.................................... mucho. Mi amiga Ana es más energética que yo: yo no*
(**4 hacer**) *.................................... mucho deporte, pero ella* (**5 practicar**) *.................................... la*
vela y el piragüismo en la montaña. El viernes por la tarde, Ana y yo
(**6 salir**) *.................................... a la discoteca o al cine.*

Speaking

Around town

50

REMEMBER After **hay**, use **un** for masculine places (**un banco**) and **una** for feminine ones (**una farmacia**). To ask if there are any toilets, use: **¿Hay servicios?**

Exploring a new place can be very confusing and it can be quicker to ask a passer-by rather than look at a map. You can just ask: **¿Hay un/una ... por aquí?** (Is there a ... near here?) and you should get the reply: **Hay uno/una en ...** (There's one in ...). Other words you might hear include **la calle** (street), **la avenida** (avenue), **la plaza** (square) and **el paseo** (wide avenue). For places on a corner, just say: **en la esquina de (la Calle ...) y (la Avenida ...).**

Contesta a las preguntas. Using the map, answer the questions.
Ejemplo: ¿Hay un banco por aquí?
– Hay uno en la Calle Goya.

1 *¿Hay una parada de autobuses por aquí?*
2 *¿Hay un estanco por aquí?*
3 *¿Hay una cafetería por aquí?*
4 *¿Hay una farmacia por aquí?*
5 *¿Hay una oficina de turismo por aquí?*

REMEMBER In the reply, **un** becomes **uno**: Hay **uno** en la Calle Goya (There's one in Goya Street).

If you want more specific instructions, ask: **¿Dónde está/están ...?** (Where is/are ...?) The reply will begin: **Está/están ...** (It's/they are ...).

See if you can now ask where all the places on the map are: **¿Dónde está el banco?**

To give an accurate reply, you need to know how to say 'in front of', 'beside' etc. Look at page 34 and refresh your memory.

Completa el diálogo. Complete the dialogue using the map above.

TURISTA	*Perdone, señora. ¿Hay un estanco ...(1)... aquí?*
SEÑORA	*Sí, hay ...(2)... en la Avenida de Cádiz.*
TURISTA	*¿Dónde está exactamente?*
SEÑORA	*Está ...(3)... del mercado, entre las tiendas turísticas y ...(4)...*
TURISTA	*Muchas ...(5)...*
SEÑORA	*De nada. Adiós.*

REMEMBER After **está** use **el** for a masculine place (**el banco**) and **la** for a feminine place (**la cafetería**). With plural nouns, use **los** if they're masculine (**los servicios**) and **las** if they're feminine (**las tiendas**).

Think up some more dialogues asking where places on the map are. Be as precise as you can in your answers.

Which way?

There are several ways you can ask for directions. The following all mean 'How do you get to ...?': **¿Para ir a ... ?** **¿Cómo ir a ...?** **¿Por dónde se va a ...?**

(?) How would you ask the way to the following places?

el banco de España
la catedral
la plaza de toros
los servicios
la playa
el centro comercial

51

REMEMBER
When a is followed by **el**, they join together to form **al**. When **de** is followed by **el**, they join together to form **del**.

If you're stopping someone in the street, it's polite to start with **perdone** (excuse me). You could also begin with: **¿Me puede decir ...?** (Could you tell me ...?) and don't forget to add **por favor** (please).

(?) See if you can now ask the way to the six places above very politely:
Perdone, ¿me puede decir por dónde se va al banco de España, por favor?

Giving the correct directions is very important. See how many you can remember with this next activity.

◎ **Pon en orden. ¿Qué significan las indicaciones?** Put the words in the right order. What do the directions mean?
Ejemplo: calle la suba
                Suba la calle. (Go up the street.)

1 la baje calle
2 izquierda a tuerza la
3 izquierda a primera la tome la
4 recto todo siga
5 calle de final al la

6 plaza cruce la
7 a tuerza derecha la
8 la a la tome derecha segunda
9 el hasta cruce
10 semáforos los hasta

Now try answering each of the questions below in Spanish, using the map on page 50 and starting from **Estás aquí.** You can include the following useful phrase once during the activity: **Lo siento, no sé. No soy de aquí.** (I'm sorry, I don't know. I'm not from around here.)

◎ **Contesta a las preguntas.** Answer the questions using the map on page 50.

REMEMBER
Don't rush your answers – take your time to think them through!

Perdone – ¿para ir al banco, por favor?

Perdone: ¿por dónde se va al Corte Inglés, por favor?

¿Por dónde se va a la oficina de turismo, por favor?

¿Para ir a la catedral?

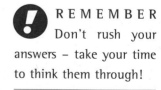

¿Me puede decir dónde están los servicios?

The World Around Us

Speaking

Tickets and travel

52

REMEMBER When you are asking for a ticket <u>to</u> a place, use the word **para**: **un billete <u>para</u> Madrid.**

There are a number of different types of ticket you can buy: **un billete de ida sólo/un billete sencillo** (single ticket) or **un billete de ida y vuelta** (return ticket). You might want a book of tickets for the bus or metro: **un carnet de (10) viajes.** You can travel **primera clase** (first class) or **segunda clase** (standard class). You might also be asked whether you want **no fumador** (non-smoking) or **fumador** (smoking).

See if you can ask for the following things.

1 single ticket to Madrid
2 non-smoking ticket
3 first class ticket
4 return ticket to Calahorra
5 two single tickets to Zaragoza
6 book of ten tickets for the bus
7 standard class ticket

As well as buying your ticket, you might also need to find out when the train or bus arrives: **¿A qué hora llega el tren/autobús?**, when it leaves: **¿A qué hora sale el tren/autobús?** and which platform it goes from: **¿De qué andén sale?** Try to work out what you need to say in the dialogue below.

REMEMBER If your prompt is in English in the exam, you don't need to work out the Spanish for these words, e.g. 'Say you'd like ...'. Imagine that someone is whispering the instruction in your ear – what you would actually say in Spanish to the ticket clerk is 'I'd like ...' (Quisiera ...).

Completa el diálogo. Complete the dialogue.

EMPLEADO/A	*Buenos días, ¿en qué puedo servirle?*
TÚ	(Say you'd like a return ticket to Toledo, non-smoking, please.)
EMPLEADO/A	*¿Qué clase?*
TÚ	(Say you'd like a standard class seat.)
EMPLEADO/A	*Tres mil pesetas.*
TÚ	(Ask when the train arrives in Toledo.)
EMPLEADO/A	*A las doce treinta.*
TÚ	(Ask which platform it leaves from.)
EMPLEADO/A	*Andén número cinco.*
TÚ	(Say thank you and goodbye.)

In the exam, you might be given picture prompts to tell you what to say. Try this dialogue. The replies in bold are the ticket clerk's. She greets you with: **Buenos días, ¿qué desea?**

Completa el diálogo. Complete the dialogue.

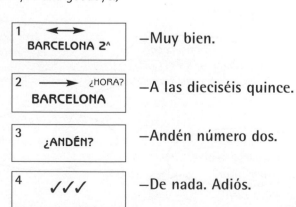

1 ← → BARCELONA 2ᴬ	—Muy bien.
2 → ¿HORA? BARCELONA	—A las dieciséis quince.
3 ¿ANDÉN?	—Andén número dos.
4 ✓✓✓	—De nada. Adiós.

Shopping for food

If you're going shopping, you'll need to know how to say the amount of the items you want, or how many packets, bottles etc.

◎ Can you find an appropriate product or foodstuff for each item in the list below? There may be several possibilities for some of them.

1 una barra de	a pan
2 una bolsa de	b tarta de manzanas
3 un bote de	c limonada
4 una botella de	d leche
5 una caja de	e cerillas
6 un kilo de	f miel
7 una lata de	g tisús
8 un litro de	h naranjas
9 un paquete de	i atún
10 un trozo de	j crema solar
11 un tubo de	k patatas fritas

(?) How many other items do you know which might match the containers and quantities above? See how many you can think of in one minute!

When you're paying for items, you might discover that you don't have any change (**lo siento, no tengo cambio**). It's polite to explain 'I've only got a (one) thousand peseta note': **Sólo tengo un billete de (mil) pesetas**. The shopkeeper will probably say it doesn't matter (**no importa**).

53

REMEMBER If you only want half a litre or half a kilo, use **medio litro/medio kilo**. Items like ham and cheese are often bought in grams: **cien gramos de …** (100 grams of …). You will sometimes hear **un cuarto de** (a quarter of a kilo) which is the same as **doscientos cincuenta gramos** (250 grams).

The World Around Us

Practice activity

Practise this dialogue with a friend. Then use the suggestions on the right to make up three more conversations by changing the underlined words.

EMPLEADO/A	Buenos días, señor(a). ¿Qué desea?
TÚ	Quisiera <u>un kilo de manzanas</u>, por favor.
EMPLEADO/A	Muy bien. ¿Algo más?
TÚ	Sí. Deme <u>una lata de sardinas</u> y <u>una botella de vino</u>.
EMPLEADO/A	Aquí tiene. ¿Es todo?
TÚ	¿Tiene <u>pan</u>?
EMPLEADO/A	Lo siento, no queda(n).
TÚ	Es todo, entonces. ¿Cuánto es?
EMPLEADO/A	Son <u>seiscientas treinta</u>.
TÚ	Lo siento, no tengo cambio. Sólo tengo un billete de <u>mil pesetas</u>.
EMPLEADO/A	No importa. Aquí tiene.
TÚ	Gracias. Adiós.
EMPLEADO/A	De nada. Adiós.

REMEMBER For single items, use **no queda** (there's none left). For plural ones, use **no quedan** (there are none left).

1k bananas
tin of tomatoes
bottle of lemonade
grapes?
only got 5000 pta. note
(Total: 455 ptas.)

½k strawberries
pot of honey
packet of sugar
milk?
only got 10.000 pta. note
(Total: 790 ptas.)

In town

The next activity is one like you might get in the exam – you're asked to read a short text and then tick three statements about it which are correct. Don't panic if you see unfamiliar words as you can use your dictionary sensibly. Don't look up the first word you don't recognise – wait, in case you can do the task without needing it.

REMEMBER
If a word ends in 's' or 'es', it might be a plural noun. If you can't find it in the dictionary, try looking it up without the 's' or 'es'.

◎ **Lee el póster y escribe ✓ al lado de cuatro frases verdaderas.**
Read the poster and put a ✓ next to the four true statements.
Ejemplo: La tienda vende ropa. ✓

1 *La tienda cierra al mediodía.*
2 *No está abierta los domingos.*
3 *Está cerrada durante dos semanas en verano.*
4 *Cierran temprano en invierno.*
5 *Se hacen arreglos en el acto.*
6 *Hay rebajas en la sección de artículos de deporte.*

> Horario verano:
> 9.00-20.30 horas
>
> Horario invierno:
> 9.00-19.00 horas
>
> Abierto sin interrupción.
> Cerrado domingos.
>
> Cierre anual (vacaciones e inventario) 1-15 agosto.
>
> Arreglos dentro de tres días.
>
> ¡¡¡ Liquidación de pantalones cortos, camisetas y zapatillas deportivas !!!

Sometimes you might get a question in the exam which brings together vocabulary from various topic areas, such as shopping, travel and transport, and places in town.

REMEMBER
Do the answers you're sure of first. Return to the others once you've done as much as you can without a dictionary.

◎ **Empareja las señales A–H con las palabras 1–9.** Match the signs A–H with the places 1–9.

1 *la zapatería*
2 *la estación de RENFE*
3 *la iglesia*
4 *el colegio*
5 *la pastelería*
6 *la estación de autobuses*
7 *los grandes almacenes*
8 *la frutería*
9 *la tintorería*

A5 ☐ ☐ ☐ ☐ ☐ ☐ ☐

A Tarta de manzana 550 ptas

B ¡Esta semana solamente! Liquidación total de sandalias

C LIMPIEZA EN SECO: DOS PRENDAS POR EL PRECIO DE UNO.

D Oferta especial ropa jóven, 5a planta

E ¡ATENCIÓN! ANDÉN NÚMERO 3 CERRADO POR OBRAS.

F Sandías frescas - ¡sólo 100 pesetas!

G Clases particulares, inglés nativo, precios especiales estudiantes

H Misas 8.00, 10.30. Vísperas 19.00.

REMEMBER
Get some extra help with your Spanish revision via the BITESIZE internet service. The address is on the back of this book. ◉

Weather

You need to be able to understand weather phrases in the present and future tenses – but that's not as difficult as it sounds! Start with the present tense: **¿Qué tiempo hace en ...?** (What's the weather like in ...?) Read the information about the climate of Ecuador and do this activity.

◎ **Escribe las letras en la casilla apropiada.** Write the letters in the appropriate box.

Costa (estación seca): `e` ☐ ☐

Sierra (estación de las lluvias): ☐ ☐ ☐

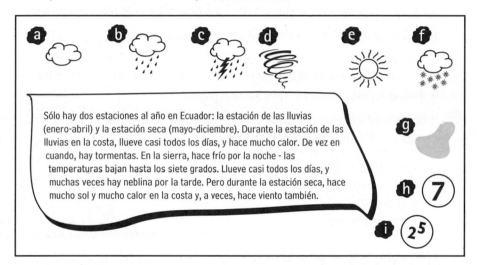

Sólo hay dos estaciones al año en Ecuador: la estación de las lluvias (enero-abril) y la estación seca (mayo-diciembre). Durante la estación de las lluvias en la costa, llueve casi todos los días, y hace mucho calor. De vez en cuando, hay tormentas. En la sierra, hace frío por la noche - las temperaturas bajan hasta los siete grados. Llueve casi todos los días, y muchas veces hay neblina por la tarde. Pero durante la estación seca, hace mucho sol y mucho calor en la costa y, a veces, hace viento también.

There are also 'families' of weather words which are useful to recognise. Rainy weather is suggested by **lloverá** (it will rain), **lluvia** (rain) and **lluvioso** (rainy). Similarly, you might come across **nubes/nubosidad** (clouds) and **nublado/nuboso** (cloudy). Other useful words are **flojo/débil** (weak/gentle) and **fuerte** (strong). Now have a go at the weather forecast below.

◎ **Completa las frases 1–5 con el nombre de la región.** Complete the sentences 1–5 with the name of the region.
Ejemplo: Tormentas en ... Andalucía.

CASTILLA Y LEÓN: continuarán hoy las temperaturas muy bajas, sobre todo en la meseta.

CANTÁBRICO: lluvias intensas y chubascos por la mañana. Sin cambio en las temperaturas.

ANDALUCÍA: las temperaturas llegarán hasta los 35 grados esta tarde. Vientos flojos del oeste.

ISLAS BALEARES: cielo despejado por la tarde, vientos más fuertes por la tarde con fenómenos tormentosos.

CATALUÑA: aumento de nubosidad por la tarde en toda la zona. Ligero descenso de temperaturas, que alcanzarán los veintidós grados.

ISLAS CANARIAS: sin cambio en las temperaturas por la mañana, con vientos fuertes del componente oeste. Más tarde, riesgo de lluvias débiles.

1 Cielo nublado en ...
2 Lloverá mucho en ...
3 Hará frío en ...
4 Hará mucho viento en ...
5 Hará muchísimo calor en ...

REMEMBER There may be information in the text which you don't need: read the question carefully to make sure you focus on the appropriate bits of the text.

55

The World Around Us

REMEMBER In weather forecasts, the verbs are usually in the future tense: **hará/será/estará** (it will be), **habrá** (there will be).

Shopping for clothes

📺 Among Spanish teenagers, shopping for clothes is as popular as in Britain.

❓ Starting at your head and working down, how many garments (**prendas**) do you know? See if you can name two things to wear on your head, something which goes around your neck, two garments for the top half of your body, two for the lower half and three items of footwear.

In the exam-type activity below, read what Amalia has to say about the clothes she likes to wear and buy. Then decide which of the three choices (a, b or c) is correct in each of the sentences. Pay attention to negative phrases which indicate 'no', 'not' or 'never'.

❗ REMEMBER
Learn these negative phrases: **no ... nunca, no ... jamás** (never), **no ... nada** (nothing), **no ... nadie** (no-one), **ni ... ni** (neither ... nor). These expressions can sometimes appear without **no: nunca llevo botas** (I never wear boots).

◎ **Lee lo que escribe Amalia y elige la frase correcta a, b o c.** Read what Amalia says and choose the correct phrase a, b or c.

1 En cuanto a ropa:
☐ *a gasta mucho dinero*
☐ *b gasta poco*
☐ *c no gasta nada.*

2 Al instituto, le gusta llevar:
☐ *a la ropa tipo sport*
☐ *b ir a la moda*
☐ *c la ropa cómoda.*

3 No le gustan las prendas de:
☐ *a nilón*
☐ *b cuero*
☐ *c algodón.*

4 Prefiere llevar los colores:
☐ *a oscuros*
☐ *b claros*
☐ *c vivos.*

5 Si va a una fiesta, prefiere la ropa:
☐ *a original*
☐ *b elegante*
☐ *c de marca.*

6 Compra en:
☐ *a los grandes almacenes*
☐ *b los boutiques*
☐ *c el mercado.*

A mi, no me interesa mucho la moda. Mis padres me dan dinero para comprar ropa, pero no gasto mucho. Entresemana cuando voy al colegio, llevo algo cómodo: vaqueros y un jersey o una camisa. Algunos de mis amigos siempre van a la moda, o llevan ropa tipo sport (chandal, con zapatillas deportivas) pero yo no. Prefiero las telas naturales, como el lino, el algodón o el cuero: nunca llevo las sintéticas, como el nilón o el poliéster.

Como soy morena, me van bien los colores alegres, como el rojo y el amarillo - no me gustan los colores tristes como el negro o el marrón, ni los aburridos como el azul claro o el color de rosa. Como no gasto mucho en ropa, no suelo llevar prendas de marca, y no soy muy original. Para salir con amigos o ir a una fiesta, me gusta ponerme una falda larga y una chaqueta. Cuando voy de compras, me gusta mirar los escaparates de los grandes almacenes, o ver lo que hay en el mercado, pero normalmente encuentro lo que busco en las tiendas pequeñas.

Tourist information

Read this letter from Mercedes about her home town.

◎ **Para cada lugar 1–8 escribe la letra del dibujo correcto a–h.**
For each place 1–8 write the letter of the correct picture a–h.

¿Qué tal? yo bien. Quieres saber algo de mi ciudad, ¿verdad? Vivo en el sur en una ciudad pequeña de la costa. La ciudad tiene unos treinta mil habitantes. Vivo en la parte antigua - es muy bonita y tiene muchas calles estrechas (1) donde se puede pasear. Mi casa está en una plaza cerca del puerto, y enfrente están el Ayuntamiento (2) y el mercado. Por la mañana, la zona es muy ruidosa, porque el mercado se abre a las seis y hay mucho tráfico (3). De interés histórico, hay la iglesia (4) de San Tomás en el centro, rodeada de bares típicos (5). Hay un castillo y en las afueras hay ruinas romanas. La ciudad tiene una piscina cerca de la playa con unos jardines preciosos (6), un polideportivo y un centro comercial muy bonito. Hay una parte moderna al otro lado del río (7), la cuál es industrial y fea. Mi madre trabaja allí en una clínica (8). Aquí en verano es muy turístico, pero en invierno es tranquilo. Me encanta mi ciudad en verano porque es divertido vivir aquí, pero en invierno es muy aburrido. ¿Qué opinas tú de tu ciudad? ¿Te gusta? ¿Por qué - o por qué no? ¡Hasta pronto!
Mercedes

---

a   b   c   d

e   f   g   h

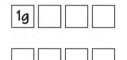

❗ REMEMBER
When matching halves of sentences, do the ones you're sure of first. Use your common sense and knowledge of grammar as well: the word **cerca**, for instance, is almost always followed by **de** or **del**.

Practice activity

Having read a letter, you might have to match halves of sentences correctly.
Try the activity below.

ⓗ Empareja correctamente las dos partes de las frases.

1 La ciudad está situada cerca ...
2 Merche vive en ...
3 Por la mañana, hay ...
4 Si te interesa la historia ...
5 La madre de Mercedes es enfermera en ...
6 En verano, vivir en la ciudad es ...

a la parte antigua.
b mucho ruido en el centro.
c del mar.
d desagradable.
e hay monumentos en las afueras.
f agradable.
g la parte moderna.

Writing

Things to do and see

(?) A word map, like the one below, is a good way of revising vocabulary. See how many words you can add to it in five minutes. Don't forget to write each noun with **un** or **una**.

REMEMBER You can make a word map to revise other topic areas. Why not make one for shopping? The three headings might be **tiendas** (shops), **productos** (products) and **frases útiles** (useful phrases).

```
De interés turístico, hay ...          Para divertirse, hay ...
un castillo                             un cine
...................        LA CIUDAD    ...................
...................                     ...................
...................   Para comprar, hay ...   ...................
...................   grandes almacenes       ...................
...................        ...................
...................        ...................
```

In the exam, you might have a letter to reply to. The writer might ask: **¿Qué hay en tu ciudad?** (What is there in your town?) As well as explaining what there is, using the language from your word map above, you can also explain what there isn't: **No hay ...**

REMEMBER After **no hay** you don't need **un** or **una**: no hay discoteca.

If you want to expand a little (and impress the examiner!), try using some of these phrases:

✗ *lo malo/lo peor/el problema es que no hay ...*
the bad thing/worst thing/the problem is that there isn't/aren't ...

✔ *lo bueno/lo mejor/lo que me gusta es que hay ...*
the good thing/the best thing/what I like is that there is/are ...

These phrases might also come in handy: **Hay mucho que hacer** (there's lots to do) and: **No hay nada que hacer** (there's nothing to do).

◎ Now try writing a few sentences, using the ideas below to help.

REMEMBER There are other phrases you can add here: **para los jóvenes** (for young people), **para niños** (for children), **para turistas** (for tourists) and **para los mayores** (for older people).

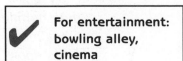 For tourists: cathedral, museum, castle

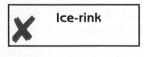 If you want to shop: shopping centre, shops near beach

For entertainment: bowling alley, cinema

Ice-rink

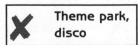 Theme park, disco

Describing your village, town or region

In the exam, you might be asked to describe your home town and area. First of all, make sure you know how to say where it is.

◎ **Rellena los huecos 1–9.** Fill in the gaps 1–9.

1 *Mi pueblo está en* .... (the coast)
2 *La ciudad está junto al* .... (river) *Tago.*
3 *El pueblo está en* .... (the countryside)
4 *Mi ciudad está situada en* .... (the mountains)
5 *Vivo en la capital en* .... (the centre) *del país.*

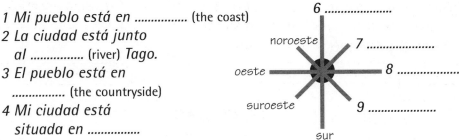

6 ....
noroeste
7 ....
oeste — 8 ....
suroeste
9 ....
sur

You might also be asked what your town or village is like: **¿Cómo es tu ciudad o pueblo?** To describe it, you'll need to use plenty of adjectives.

◎ Can you sort these adjectives into two lists? The endings will give you a clue.

El pueblo es ...	La ciudad es ...
bonito	

fea   *pequeña*
bonito   *turístico*
acogedor   *animada*
antiguo   *moderna*
aburrida   *tranquilo*
ruidosa   *histórico*

> **! R E M E M B E R**
> Adjectives ending in 'o' in the masculine form change to 'a' in the feminine. The following adjectives stay the same for both: **industrial, interesante, alegre, grande.**

You should be able to write some sentences to describe your home town or village now. Don't forget to change the endings on the adjectives if necessary: **Mi ciudad es antigua ...**

◎ **¿Cómo es tu ciudad o pueblo?** What's your town or village like?

Practice activity

Try writing a longer description of your own home town or village and area. Read Miguel's letter and change the underlined words and expressions as necessary for your own text.

ⓗ Escribe sobre tu ciudad o pueblo.

¡Hola! Me llamo Miguel y vivo en el <u>norte de Colombia</u>. Mi ciudad se llama <u>Cartagena</u>. De interés turístico, hay <u>la parte antigua, la catedral y el Palacio de la Inquisición</u>. Para comprar, hay <u>las tiendas turísticas y un mercado</u>. Par divertirse, están <u>la playa, la fiesta (en marzo) y muchos clubs y discotecas</u>. ¿Cómo es la ciudad? Es <u>histórica y bonita</u>, pero también <u>ruidosa</u> y un poco <u>sucia</u>. ¿Y la región? Por un lado hay mucho <u>turismo</u> y mucho <u>comercio</u>; por otro, en algunas zonas hay mucho <u>desempleo</u>. Lo bueno es que hay <u>mucho campo bonito</u>, pero el problema es que no hay <u>mucho para los jóvenes en los pueblos</u>.

The World of Work

This section is about

- Jobs
- Work experience
- Future plans
- Communications

This section is all about the world of work: jobs, including part-time work, what your work experience was like, what you plan to do after the exams and what you might like to do in the future. It also includes work-related communications, such as using the phone.

Jobs

As women become an increasingly vital part of the workforce and do a much wider variety of jobs (**empleos**) than before, the Spanish have had to adapt the names of occupations traditionally done by men, to show that they are now done by women too. Part-time jobs for young people under the age of sixteen are not always easy to come by, but some work in family businesses (**negocios**) at the weekends or in the holidays.

Work experience

Work experience in Spain is known as **la experiencia laboral** or **las prácticas de trabajo**. If you've done work experience, with any luck, your boss was nice (**mi jefe/a era simpático/a**) and you had a great time (**¡lo pasé bomba!**), but you might have found the work only just bearable (**soportable**) or downright boring (**aburrido**) at times!

Future plans

Spanish teenagers also sit an exam at the age of 16 which is called BUP (**Bachillerato Unificado Polivalente**) and afterwards many stay on at school to do the COU exam (**Curso de Orientación Universitaria**) which prepares them for going to university. They may also opt to do a more practical course in a technical college (**Escuela Técnica Superior**). The majority of students go to their nearest university and continue living at home, as the costs of moving away can be too much. Although courses normally last between three and five years, some students do postgraduate study, as competition for jobs is keen.

Communications

The Spanish are keen users of modern technology, and if you have access to the Internet, try and find some Spanish or South American websites (**páginas de web**). You might be able to join a special interest group and 'chat' to some young people – a great way to improve your Spanish! Talking on the phone in a foreign language can be a nerve-wracking task (even for adults), but once you've worked your way through the activities, you'll feel more confident about taking part in a phone conversation. So let's get started – **¡vámonos!**

◎ These phrases will be really useful for your exam, so see if you can try and learn them!

Jobs

¿En qué trabaja tu madre?
What does your mother do?

¿Qué tipo de trabajo hace tu padrastro?
What work does your stepfather do?

*Es cartero/a, enfermero/a, dentista,
funcionario, maestro/a.*
He/she's a post-person, nurse, dentist,
civil servant, primary school teacher.

Trabajo, trabaja en ...
I work, he/she works in ...

una oficina, una fábrica, una tienda, en casa
an office, a factory, a shop, at home

Work experience

¿Dónde hiciste tus prácticas de trabajo?
Where did you do your work experience?

Trabajé en ...   I worked in ...

¿Qué tenías que hacer?
What did you have to do?

Tenía que ...   I had to ...

archivar, escribir a máquina, hacer el café
do the filing, type, make the coffee

hacer recados, hacer pedidos, mandar faxes
run errands, take orders, send faxes

responder a consultas del público
answer queries from the public

*usar/utilizar el ordenador, mandar cartas por
correo electrónico*
use the computer, send letters by e-mail

¿Te gustó el trabajo?
Did you like the work?

Era ... soportable, interesante, divertido.
It was ... bearable, interesting, fun.

Lo encontré ... aburrido, repetitivo, estresante.
I found it ... boring, repetitive, stressful.

Future plans

¿Qué planes tienes para el futuro?
What plans do you have for the future?

¿Qué quieres hacer el añó que viene?
What do you want to do next year?

¿En qué te gustaría trabajar?   What kind of
work would you like to do?

*Quiero/quisiera/espero/tengo la intención
de ...*   I want to/I'd like to/I hope to/
I plan to ...

seguir estudiando, ir a la universidad
carry on studying, go to university

buscar un trabajo/trabajar en ...
look for a job/work in ...

el sector del turismo/del comercio
tourism/business

la hostelería   the hotel and catering industry

la enseñanza/los servicios médicos
teaching/medical services

Communications

¿Qué tengo que hacer para ...?
What do I have to do to ...?

mandar un fax/algo por correo electrónico
send a fax/an e-mail

llamar a casa/a Gran Bretaña
phone home/Great Britain

¿Puedo hablar con ...?/¿Me pone con ...?
Can I speak to ...?

Lo siento, no está.
I'm sorry, he/she isn't here.

¿Quiere(s) dejar un recado?
Do you want to leave a message?

¿Puedo dejar un recado?
Can I leave a message?

Volveré a llamar más tarde.   I'll ring later.

Future plans

In the exam, you might have to listen for, and write, specific words in sentences or texts. This means that you have to listen very carefully for individual words. The first thing to do is to read the gapped text and familiarise yourself with what you'll hear once the tape starts. Next, try and work out what kind of word you might hear which will make sense.

Read what Virginia has to say below about her and her friends' plans for the future, and see if you can match each numbered gap to one of the following: a place, a school subject, an adjective, a number, a verb.

A los ...(1)... años tenemos que hacer los exámenes más importantes porque tenemos que ...(2)... para poder ir a la universidad. Como quiero ser profesora de ...(3)... tendré que hacer tres años de curso universitario. Todos mis amigos quieren ir a la ...(4)... porque quieren conseguir un ...(5)... empleo en el futuro.

Now find the clip where Virginia introduces her and her friends' plans for the future and do the following activity.

Escucha y rellena los huecos de arriba. Listen and fill in the gaps above.

As you probably know already, there's often more than one way of saying something. Listening activities often test this, so try the activity below for practice. Find the clip which begins with Maite asking her friends: **¿Dónde vas a ir para seguir tus estudios?** (Where are you going to go to carry on your studies?) Read the speech bubbles through before you watch the clip.

Escucha y escribe cada letra A–F al lado de la persona apropiada. Listen and write each letter A–F beside the appropriate person.
Ejemplo: Chica 1 = C, ...

Chica 1: ....
Bachir: ....
Chica 2: ....
Chico 1: ....

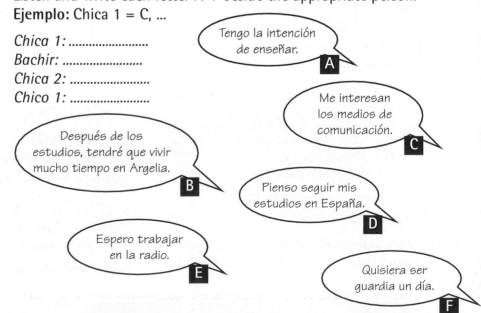

Tengo la intención de enseñar. **A**

Me interesan los medios de comunicación. **C**

Después de los estudios, tendré que vivir mucho tiempo en Argelia. **B**

Pienso seguir mis estudios en España. **D**

Espero trabajar en la radio. **E**

Quisiera ser guardia un día. **F**

Jobs and careers

Deciding on a job or career is not always easy. Find the clip which begins: Y tu qué quieres hacer en el futuro?, in which Virginia's friends talk about their plans. Listen to the first five of them, and find the most appropriate thought-bubble (A–F) for each.

◉ **Para cada persona, escribe la letra más adecuada. Sobra una.** for each person, write the most appropriate letter. there will be one left over.

1 Remedios ☐

2 Begoña ☐

3 David ☐

4 Nuria ☐

5 Marcos ☐

A — Ser dueño/a de una casa discográfica.

B — Quiero tener un empleo físco.

C — Voy a tener una escuela de idiomas extranjeros.

D — Espero ser miembro del gobierno un día.

E — Un día, voy a escribir un libro sobre la Guerra Civil.

F — Me gustaría ser dueño de un periódico.

❗ REMEMBER
You won't always hear the same words on tape as are on the page: try and understand the meaning of what people are saying.

Practice activity

At Higher level, you will almost certainly have to do an activity in which you are asked to identify opinions and emotions. Find the clip where Isabel and Carmen talk about their exams, then read the questions below carefully. Make sure you are clear to which person (Isabel or Carmen) each one relates. Now play the tape and do the activity.

🎧 **Escucha la conversacíon. Escribe ✓ en las casillas apropriadas.**

1 En cuanto a los exámenes, Isabel se muestra ...
 a) llena de entusiasmo ☐
 b) bastante positiva ☐
 c) negativa ☐

2 ¿Qué opina Isabel de la moda?
 a) no la toma muy en serio ☐
 b) le interesa mucho ☐
 c) le parece una tontería ☐

3 Un día, Carmen espera ser ...
 a) directora ☐
 b) diseñadora ☐
 c) modelo ☐

4 Por lo que se refiere a los exámenes ...
 a) a Carmen le da igual ☐
 b) Carmen va a suspender ☐
 c) Carmen quiere aprobar ☐

5 En cuanto a la carrera, Isabel ...
 a) no sabe lo que quiere hacer ☐
 b) quiere trabajar en la moda ☐
 c) no quiere seguir estudiando ☐

6 ¿Cómo se siente Isabel?
 a) enfadada ☐
 b) deprimida ☐
 c) alegre ☐

The World of Work

Speaking

Leaving phone messages

You might have to do a role-play in the exam where you're making a phone call. Perhaps you're arranging to go out or leaving a message for someone. What sort of things do you say to someone on the phone that you don't say face to face?

In Spain, when you pick up a ringing phone you would usually say: **¿Diga?** This means, literally, 'tell me' – a signal that you're there. In reply, the caller says **¡Oiga!** which means 'listen!' If you want to give your name, start with: **Soy (Jessica)** and if you want to ask for someone, say: **¿Está (Marcos)?** If you want to leave a message, ask: **¿Puedo dejar un recado?** You could follow that with: **Dile que volveré a llamar a ...** (Tell him/her that I'll call back at ...) When you're saying goodbye, there are a number of possibilities: **Hasta luego, Hasta pronto** or – if you're phoning back tomorrow – **Hasta mañana**.

◎ Now try putting all that together! Work out what you would say in Spanish if you were playing role B in the phone conversation below.

A	B
¿Diga?	*1* Reply.
¡Hola! Soy Juan.	*2* Ask if Ana is there.
Lo siento, no está.	*3* Ask if you can leave a message.
Claro.	*4* Explain that you'll ring later, about nine.
Muy bien. ¿De parte de quién?	*5* Give your name.
Vale.	*6* Say thank you and goodbye.
Adiós.	

It might be that you have a more formal phone call to make. Try this next activity where you have to find the correct reply (a–h) to each of the receptionist's responses 1–8. See also if you can spot the Spanish for: 'I'm sorry, the line's busy', 'the STD code', 'Can you put me through to ...?' and 'Can he/she ring me at ...?'

◎ **Empareja a–h con 1–8.** Match a–h to 1–8.

1 Hotel Santa Fé, ¿dígame?
2 Sí. ¿En qué puedo servirle?
3 Momento ... Lo siento, está comunicando.
4 ¿Quiere dejar un recado?
5 A las cinco. Muy bien. ¿De parte de quién?
6 ¿Cuál es su número de teléfono, señor Brown?
7 ¿Y cuál es el prefijo de la ciudad?
8 Muchas gracias, señor. Se lo diré.

a Soy Jason Brown, de Inglaterra.

b Es el 62 42 98.

c Muchas gracias. Hasta luego.

d Vale. ¿Me puede llamar a las cinco?

e Buenas tardes. ¿Hablo con la recepcionista?

f ¡Ah! ¡Qué fastidia!

g Es el 0298.

h ¿Me pone con la Señorita Jiménez, por favor?

! REMEMBER If you want to give an approximate time, use **a eso de** or **alrededor de**: **a eso de las diez** means 'about ten'.

! REMEMBER Spanish phone numbers are given in pairs: 54 20 12 is **cincuenta y cuatro, veinte, doce**. Where there's a group of three at the start (430), the first one is given on its own: **cuatro, treinta ...**

Part-time jobs

In the conversation part of the exam, you might be asked if you have got a part-time job – perhaps you work for a few hours after school each day or on Saturdays or just in the holidays.

(?) Read through this sample conversation. What do you notice about the length of the student's replies?

PROFESOR/A	ESTUDIANTE
¿Tienes algún empleo?	*Sí. Trabajo en un garaje.*
¿Cuándo trabajas?	*Trabajo los sábados.*
¿Cuántas horas trabajas?	*Trabajo siete horas.*
¿Cuándo empiezas?	*Empiezo a las nueve de la mañana.*
¿Cuándo terminas?	*Termino a las cuatro de la tarde.*
¿Cuánto ganas?	*Gano ochocientas pesetas por hora.*
¿Qué opinas del trabajo?	*Me gusta – es interesante.*

They're all very short. The teacher or examiner does nearly as much talking as the student does and he/she has to ask lots of questions in order to get all the information. It's much better if you are able to say several things in reply to a question, so that the teacher or examiner's voice is heard less than yours.

See if you can give a fuller answer than the student above – you can use the information given above to fill in the gaps below.

(◎) **Rellena los huecos.** Fill in the gaps.

PROFESOR/A	ESTUDIANTE
¿Tienes algún empleo?	*Sí. Trabajo en un garaje los ...(1)...*
¿Cuándo trabajas?	*Trabajo ...(2)... horas en general: empiezo a las ...(3)... de la mañana, y termino a las ...(4)... de la tarde, en general.*
¿Cuánto ganas?	*Gano ...(5)... pesetas por hora. No está mal, y me gusta el trabajo. Es ...(6)...*

Use the dialogue above as a model to help you work out further dialogues about part-time jobs. Make sure that you say more than the teacher or examiner!

(◎) **Inventa tres conversaciones.** Make up three more interviews.

1
- supermercado
- lunes–viernes
- 18.00–21.00
- 750 ptas p.h
- ✓✓

2
- restaurante
- sáb. + dom.
- 11.00–17.00
- 700 ptas p.h.
- xx

3
- peluquería
- sábado
- 8.00–17.30
- 650 ptas p.h.
- ✓✓

! REMEMBER
The speaking part of the exam will almost certainly be recorded. If your teacher or the examiner has to ask you lots of questions, then there's less time left on the tape for you to show what you can say. Try and give several pieces of information in reply to each question.

! REMEMBER
If you want to say that you work on Saturdays, for example, say **los (sábados)**. If you just work in the morning, add **por la mañana** and if your job is in the afternoon or evening, add **por la tarde**. If you work every day from Monday to Friday, use **de lunes a viernes**.

The World of Work

Speaking

Work experience

In the conversation part of the exam, you might have to give details of your work experience – **la experiencia laboral** or **las prácticas de trabajo** in Spanish. You'll need to understand the information you're being asked for.

◎ Start off by matching the questions 1–8 with the Spanish equivalents a–h in the conversation at the bottom of the page.

1 *What were your hours like?*
2 *How did you get to work?*
3 *When was the lunch break?*
4 *Where did you do your work experience?*
5 *Were there any breaks?*
6 *How long did it take to get there?*
7 *Did you like the work?*
8 *How long did your work experience last?*

It's important to give as much detail as you can, but a lot of the vocabulary will already be familiar from other topic areas, such as travel and transport, talking about getting to and from school and your school timetable. Make sure that you can give an opinion on your work experience and try to find something positive to say. Even if the work was **repetitivo** (repetitive) or **mi jefe/a era pesado/a** (my boss was a pain), your workmates were probably nice: **Mis compañeros eran simpáticos.**

! REMEMBER You need to learn the Spanish for the type of questions you might be asked on a topic: if you give a reply to a question you weren't asked, you won't get any marks!

! REMEMBER Try and use some of the following expressions to add colour and variety to what you say: **para decir la verdad** (to tell the truth), **francamente** (frankly), **en realidad** (in fact), **en general** (on the whole) or **a veces/de vez en cuando** (sometimes).

◎ Practise saying the dialogue below, then make up one using the suggestions on the right.

a *¿Dónde hiciste tu experiencia laboral?*
   Trabajé en un laboratorio.
b *¿Cuánto tiempo duraron las prácticas?*
   Duraron quince días.
c *¿Cómo ibas al trabajo?*
   Iba en metro.
d *¿Cuánto tiempo tardabas en llegar?*
   Tardaba unos treinta minutos.
e *¿Cómo era tu horario?*
   Trabajaba desde las ocho hasta las cuatro.
f *¿Había descansos?*
   Sí. Había dos descansos de quince minutos.
g *¿Cuándo era la hora de comer?*
   Era de doce a una.
h *¿Te gustó el trabajo?*
   Sí. En general, era bastante interesante pero a veces era aburrido.

> **WORK EXPERIENCE**
> 10 days – travel agents
> Went by bus and on foot – took nearly an hour!
> Hours: 9–5.30, with lunch from 1–2
> Breaks: 3 x 20 mins
> Great fun on the whole, but a bit repetitive sometimes

◎ **Habla de tu experiencia laboral.** Talk about your work experience.

The world of work

As part of the exam, you might have to give a presentation on a topic of your choice. The world of work can be a good one to choose as it offers you the opportunity to use a range of tenses.

To start off, make notes for yourself, like the ones below. There may be other things you want to add: perhaps you had a summer job last year and you could talk about that in the 'Work experience' section or you'd like to say something about the advantages and disadvantages of different types of jobs in 'Future plans'.

Part-time job
• where I work
• the hours
• how much I earn
• what I think of it
(PRESENT TENSE)

Work experience
• where I worked
• getting there
• what I had to do
• my opinion
(PAST TENSE)

Future plans
• what I plan to do after the exams
• what kind of job I want and why
(FUTURE TENSE)

> **! REMEMBER** To gain a higher grade, you need to be able to show you can use a variety of tenses (past, present and future) and give your opinion.

Now work out what you want to say in Spanish on each of these topics. It helps to write it down or do it on a computer so that you can add things or alter bits easily. The list of verbs below will help you use a mixture of tenses. Where it says (infin.), you need to use an infinitive. For example: **suelo trabajar** (I usually work), **tenía que coger el teléfono** (I had to answer the phone) and **espero seguir estudiando** (I hope to carry on studying).

Present tense
• trabajo – I work
• gano – I earn
• empiezo – I start
• me gusta – I like
• termino – I finish
• suelo (infin.) – I usually

Past tense
• trabajé – I worked
• fui allí – I went there
• empezaba – I started
• me gustaba – I liked
• terminaba – I finished
• tenía que (infin.) – I had to

Future tense
• voy a (infin.) – I'm going to
• tengo la intención de (infin.) – I plan to
• quisiera (infin.) – I'd like to
• iré – I will go
• espero (infin.) – I hope to
• pienso (infin.) – I'm thinking of

> **! REMEMBER** You can't read from your notes when giving a presentation, but you are allowed several postcard-sized pieces of paper with a few headings in Spanish on each one to prompt you.

Don't forget to give your opinion: use **es** for 'it is' and **era** for 'it was'. You might like to add: **Lo pasé muy bien/mal** (I had a great/horrible time), **Me divertí mucho** (I really enjoyed it) or **Me aburrí un montón** (I was really bored).

Practice activity

It's a good idea to start preparing your presentation early, and keep updating it with extra phrases as you revise. Your teacher or a student in the Sixth Form might be able to give you some help and advice.

If you make notes on the computer, you can keep on updating your work as you think of more ideas and phrases to use. Make a start now, by preparing a presentation on your own work experience.

Forms

In the exam, you might be asked to show you understand a CV or you might have to write one yourself. The headings on this CV could also be useful if you have to fill in an ID form, an application form or a booking request.

◎ **Rellena el formulario con los detalles de abajo.** Complete the form with the details below.

! REMEMBER Forms ask for surnames (apellidos), because the Spanish have two: the father's surname and the mother's.

! REMEMBER All Spanish citizens have to carry an identity card: **un documento nacional de identidad (D.N.I.).** You would need to give your passport number if asked.

! REMEMBER Fill in the details you're sure of first, then look at what's left over and make sensible guesses as to what goes on the other lines.

CURRICULUM VITAE

1 Apellidos: ....

2 Nombre: ....

3 Edad: ....

4 Fecha de nacimiento: ....

5 Lugar de nacimiento: ....

6 Nacionalidad: ....

7 Estado civil: ....

8 D.N.I./Pasaporte: ....

9 Dirección (+ código postal): ....

10 Teléfono: ....

11 Estudios: ....

12 Cargos que ha ejercido: ....

13 Pasatiempos: ....

14 Empleo ideal: ....

Instituto San Ignacio, Madrid (BUP, COU)

Fotografía/baloncesto   (91) 746 65 71

Médico   Lima, Perú.   Soltera

Carmen   Calle San Agustín, 18, 2ºD, 28002, Madrid

Prácticas de trabajo en el Hospital Juan de Dios

Peruana   10-4-1982   36 741 802C

17 años   García Morales

Job adverts

In the next activity, you'll be reading four short adverts. Don't worry if you don't understand every word!

(?) First, scan the texts which you have to match up. Can you see any similarities between any of the words in the speech bubbles and the words in the adverts? For example, **hermanas** might be connected to **hijos**. What other connections can you find?

(!) R E M E M B E R
On the exam paper, you can underline things, draw arrows to relevant information and scribble notes – it's not like a textbook in class!

> Me gustaría trabajar en el sector del turismo o de la hostelería durante el verano. El año pasado, pasé tres meses trabajando como ayudante general en la recepción del hostal de mi tía.

Begoña

> Soy el mayor, y tengo que cuidar a mis dos hermanas de cuatro y siete años después de las clases, y los sábados. El año pasado, trabajé como monitor en la guardería de un hotel.

Juanjo

> Entresemana, de las cinco de la tarde hasta las nueve, trabajo en la tienda del polideportivo o en el gimnasio. Durante el verano que viene, quisiera buscar un empleo que pueda hacer los sábados y domingos solamente.

David

1
BUSCAMOS:
chico/a para ayudar a padres con dos hijos (2 y 6) durante los meses de verano.
Experiencia deseable.
Tel. (91) 592 61 44

4
Se busca: personal para temporada julio-septiembre.
HOTEL-RESIDENCIA EL ALMIRANTE.
Camareros/as, recepcionistas, limpieza.
Tel: (91) 238 91 61

2
▶ ¿Le interesa para el verano en la playa? Buscamos jóvenes con experiencia para camping Costa Verde: montar tiendas y ayudar en la oficina de información.
Interesados llamar
✆ **(91) 380 43 29**

DEPORTE JOVEN:
chico/a para fines de semana.
Ayudar en almacén.
Buena voluntad más importante que experiencia.
Tel. (91) 296 23 59 **3**

(!) R E M E M B E R
Once you think you've got the answers, read the text which is left over and compare it to each speech bubble in turn, just to make sure.

(◎) Para cada joven, busca el anuncio más apropiado. Find the most appropriate advert for each young person.

Begoña ☐   David ☐   Juanjo ☐

The World of Work

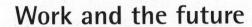
Work and the future

The Practice activity below is an example of another type of task you might get in the exam. You have to read a passage and then copy out the relevant phrase in Spanish for each sentence which follows it. In this type of task, you need to be careful about tenses – some sentences might refer to the past or future, so be sure that you select the correct piece of information.

As preparation, read the sentences 1–8 in the Practice activity below and note beside each one whether it refers to the past (PT), present (PS) or future (F).

REMEMBER
When reading the text, you might find it helpful to underline those verbs which indicate the past and circle the ones which point to the future. Don't forget to look for clues like **el año pasado** (last year) and **el año próximo** (next year).

¡Hola! Me llamo Manolo y estoy en el tercero de BUP. Voy al instituto todos los días, pero también tengo dos empleos. Los sábados y domingos ayudo a mi tío en su taller - es mecánico. De lunes a viernes, trabajo como dependiente en una frutería cerca de casa. El año pasado hice mis prácticas de trabajo en una oficina de información y turismo. Pasé ocho días laborables allí, y me divertí mucho. Tenía que tratar con el público, lo que me gustaba mucho. Pero mejor todavía era preparar folletos turísticos en el ordenador. Después de los exámenes hay la posibilidad de tener un empleo en la misma oficina, pero creo que quiero seguir estudiando el año próximo y hacer el COU. Como carrera, me interesa mucho el sector del turismo pero, según mi padre, sería mejor hacer algo más práctico, como tener mi propio negocio. Pero no estoy seguro - me gusta mucho ayudar a la gente. ¿Quién sabe? También quisiera viajar al extranjero. El año pasado, fui a México con mi familia, lo qué me encantó, y tal vez un día iré a vivir en otro país sudamericano como Bolivia o el Perú.

Practice activity

h Lee la carta de Manolo y copia la frase que indica ...

1 ... qué tipo de trabajo hace Manolo entresemana.
2 ... dónde trabaja los fines de semana.
3 ... cuánto tiempo duró su experiencia laboral.
4 ... lo que más le gustó de su experiencia.
5 ... qué quiere hacer el año académico que viene.
6 ... qué tipo de trabajo quiere hacer en el futuro.
7 ... por qué le gustaría hacerlo.
8 ... dónde vivirá un día.

GrammarZONE

It will really improve the quality of your writing and speaking if you can use different tenses confidently. This section concentrates on the **yo** (I) form, because that's the one you'll need most often when talking about yourself. The most useful tenses for you to learn and understand are the PRETERITE, the IMPERFECT and the FUTURE.

PRETERITE	IMPERFECT	FUTURE
what happened in the past (now over and finished with)	what you used to do/were doing over a period of time	what you will do
		'I will buy/eat/go'
'I bought', 'I ate', 'I went'	*'I used to buy/eat/go'* *'I was buying/eating/going'*	

When you're talking about the things you did on work experience, use the imperfect tense because you did them over a period of time (even though you're not doing them now).

Each of these three tenses is formed by using the infinitive of the verb. The box below shows that for the preterite and imperfect tenses, you take off the **–ar, –er, –ir** ending and add the correct ending, but you don't in the future tense.

		PRETERITE	IMPERFECT	FUTURE
-ar	*trabajar (to work)*	trabajé	trabajaba	trabajaré
-er	*comer (to eat)*	comí	comía	comeré
-ir	*vivir (to live)*	viví	vivía	viviré

◎ Can you match up these Spanish phrases with their correct meanings?

1 Trabajé en una oficina.	*a I ate in the canteen yesterday.*
2 Comía en la cantina todos los días.	*b I will work in an office.*
3 Trabajaré en una oficina.	*c I will live abroad.*
4 Viviré en el extranjero.	*d I used to live in the south of Spain.*
5 Comí en la cantina ayer.	*e I worked in an office.*
6 Vivía en el sur de España.	*f I used to eat in the canteen every day.*

Some common verbs are irregular, so make sure you learn the **yo** form of these verbs:

		PRETERITE	IMPERFECT	FUTURE
hacer	*(to do, make)*	hice	hacía	haré
ir	*(to go)*	fui	iba	iré
ser	*(to be)*	fui	era*	seré
tener que	*(to have to)*	tuve que	tenía que	tendré que

* you can also use 'era' to mean 'it was ...'

◎ Now translate these sentences into Spanish.
1 I did my work experience in an office.
2 I used to go by bus.
3 I had to do the filing and make the coffee.
4 It was a bit boring and repetitive.
5 I won't (= will not) work in an office in the future.
6 I will go abroad if possible.

Writing

Jobs

You'll need to be able to recognise and spell the words for different jobs in Spanish, both for men and women. You might need to explain what your parents or carers do, or to say what kind of job you'd like in the future.

As a result of the move to promote equal opportunities for women and men in the workplace in Spain, there have been changes in the language used to describe jobs in recent years. A number of jobs which were traditionally done by men, such as **un médico** (a doctor), have needed a feminine form to show that they are now also done by women. In some cases, **una** has simply been put in front: **una médico** (a female doctor). In other cases, an alternative -**a** ending has been provided. You'll see from the table below that, for instance, a female lawyer can be either **una abogado** or **una abogada**. See if you can complete the table now – you can use a dictionary to check the male forms if you need to.

◎ **Rellena la tabla con la información correcta.** Fill in the table with the correct information.

MALE	FEMALE	ENGLISH
1	*una estudiante*	*a student*
2	*una cantante*	
3	*una fotógrafa*	
4	*una enfermera*	
5	*una profesora*	
6	*una programadora*	
7	*una dependienta*	
8	*una abogado/a*	
9	*una comerciante/a*	
10	*una ingeniero/a*	
11	*una médico*	

◎ Now write a few sentences to describe what your parents or carers do, and any older brothers or sisters. Add a sentence to say what you want to be in the future: **Un día, quiero ser ...**

Writing a CV

It's always worth taking a few moments to think through a writing activity before you put pen to paper. In the next activity, you need to think of suitable headings for a CV and then complete it with your own details. You will almost certainly have had practice at doing this in English, and exactly the same type of information needs to go into a Spanish form. First, in rough, jot down possible headings and then think about a logical order for them – your name and personal details, such as date of birth and nationality, should come before your address and phone number, with information about your education and work experience coming next. Your leisure interests and any other skills can be added at the end.

◎ **Prepara tu propio curriculum vitae.** Prepare your own curriculum vitae.

CURRICULUM VITAE

_____

_____

_____

_____

_____

_____

_____

_____

_____

_____

_____

_____

_____

_____

_____

_____

_____

Check your completed CV against the one on page 68 to see if it's at all similar.

Check your completed CV against the one on page 68

REMEMBER Always read the instruction carefully. Here, you're asked to fill in both the headings and your own information, but you might simply be asked in the exam to make a list of suitable headings.

73

REMEMBER Don't panic if you see a large empty space on the exam paper which needs filling with Spanish words! Take your time: read the instructions carefully, work out what you need to write and then start filling the space.

REMEMBER Write neatly – neither the examiner nor a potential employer will be happy with a scrawl!

The World of Work

Writing

Applying for a holiday job

Sometime in the future, you might like to try and find a summer job in Spain – so tackling this activity will not just be useful for the exam. You might have to write a formal letter of application, explaining why you would like the job and giving your potential employer details of any previous work you have done, as well as any languages you speak.

◎ **Lee la carta y rellena los huecos.** Read the letter and for each gap write the correct word in Spanish.

1 four
2 campsite
3 posts
4 summer
5 language
6 subjects
7 fairly
8 useful
9 children
10 responsible
11 to begin
12 the end

> 62 Barnham Way,
> Glasgow,
> Escocia,
> 16 de marzo
>
> Muy señor mío:
> Acabo de ver su anuncio de plazas vacantes para ...(1)... monitores en el ...(2)... Arenas Doradas en su página de web, y quiero solicitar uno de estos ....(3)....
>
> Me gustaría trabajar en España durante el ...(4)... que viene, para mejorar mis conocimientos de la ...(5)... española. El español es una de las ocho ...(6)... que estudio para los exámenes de GCSE (equivalente al BUP en España) en junio. Lo entiendo muy bien y lo hablo ...(7)... bien. También tengo algunos conocimientos del francés, lo que será muy ...(8)... en un camping situado cerca de la frontera con Francia.
>
> El año pasado, trabajé como monitora en un hotel en el oeste de Escocia. Me llevo muy bien con ...(9)..., y soy muy cortés y ...(10).... Le puedo dar los nombres de las entidades que me han empleado, si los quiere. Estaré disponible para ...(11)... a trabajar a mediados de julio y puedo seguir trabajando hasta ...(12)... de septiembre.
>
> Quedo a la espera de sus gratas noticias,
> le saluda atentamente,
> Janice Armstrong

Did you notice how to write the date, how to say 'Dear Sir' and how to finish a formal letter correctly? Now try writing one of your own in response to this advert from a magazine. Use Janice's letter above as a model.

◎ **Escribe una carta al Hotel Espléndido.** Write a letter to Hotel Espléndido.

> **Hotel Espléndido**, Paseo Marítimo, MALAGA: buscamos camareros/as y ayudantes generales (piscina, guardería), verano julio–septiembre.

REMEMBER If you're looking up a word in the dictionary and you need to make it plural (more than one) remember the general rule for forming plurals. If the word ends in a vowel (a, e, i, o, u) add 's'; if it ends in a consonant (all other letters) add 'es'.

REMEMBER If you get a model letter in the exam, read it carefully. You might be able to adapt parts of it, and it will certainly give you some ideas – but don't copy whole chunks from it.

Future plans

📺 When talking about your plans for next year and beyond, you'll need to use a future tense. The simple future involves using **voy a** (I'm going to) followed by an infinitive.

❓ Can you work out how to say the sentences 1–6 in Spanish, using the boxes A, B and C to help you? For example, the first one is: **Quiero trabajar en la enseñanza con niños pequeños.**

75

> I want to work in teaching, with small children. **1**

A
voy a
quiero
quisiera
me gustaría

B
buscar   ir   hacer
estudiar   seguir
trabajar   tener
tratar   viajar

> I'm going to carry on studying at school. **2**

> I'd like to look for a manual job. **3**

> I'd like to have my own business. **4**

C
a la universidad
estudiando en el colegio
en el sector de la industria
en los servicios médicos
en el sector del turismo
en el comercio
en la enseñanza
un empleo manual/físico
un empleo artístico/académico
con niños (pequeños)
con el público
con los animales
en equipo
en la investigación
mi propia empresa
en el extranjero
en la ingenería
en la hostelería

> I want to travel abroad. **5**

> I'd like to work in a team, in the medical services. **6**

! REMEMBER Setting yourself short tasks when you're revising is often more productive than staring at page after page of notes or vocabulary. Why not see how many sentences you can make from boxes A–C within five minutes?

! REMEMBER You can bring language from other topics here. You might like to talk about your strengths at school to explain what you want to do in the future: **Soy fuerte en ciencias y saco muy buenas notas. Por eso** (for this reason)**, me gustaría trabajar en la investigación.**

Try to use a few examples of the pure future, so that the examiner is impressed! This tense indicates 'I will (e.g. study)'. It's easy to form – just take the infinitives from box B above and add **'é'** on the end: **Buscaré un empleo artístico** (I will look for an artistic job). The only exceptions in that list are the verbs **hacer** (to do, make) which becomes **haré** and **tener** (to have) which becomes **tendré**.

Practice activity

ℎ Can you use a mixture of the simple future and the pure future to say what you are going to do next year, and as a possible job or career? Try to write two paragraphs, one beginning **El año que viene ...** (next year) and one beginning **Un día ...** (one day).

El año que viene, quiero seguir estudiando en el colegio. Voy a hacer un curso de GNVQ, y luego ir a la universidad, si puedo. En las vacaciones quiero buscar un empleo para ganar un poco de dinero. Saco buenas notas en general en las ciencias, y me gustan mucho las matemáticas – creo que me gustaría una carrera en el sector de la industria o en el comercio, o tal vez iré al extranjero ...

The World of Work

The International World

This section is about

- The international world
- Tourism
- Holiday accommodation
- The environment

This section is all about the international world: that includes holidays and trips abroad, countries you might visit and places you might stay and the environment. These are all topics you need to know about for your exam.

Countries and holidays

Have you ever visited Spain or a Spanish-speaking country? Don't forget that Spanish is a very useful language – it's not just spoken in Spain, but also in most South American countries as well. Some states in the USA are also bilingual (US-English/Spanish).

It might seem as if Spanish students have a lot of holidays: they often finish for the summer in June and don't return until the second week in September. Although they don't have any half-term breaks, they do get several feast days. If there's a fiesta on a Thursday and one the following Monday, it's common to take Friday off as well to make a long weekend of it! This is known as **hacer puente** (literally, 'making a bridge').

Where do the Spanish go on holiday? Their own Canary Islands are popular, as is Portugal. Many travel to France and Italy, with Britain being a common destination for teenagers wanting to study English. A number of families have connections with South America, so trips to see relatives there are also popular.

Tourism and the environment

Spain has long been a favourite holiday destination and the number of tourists to the Spanish-speaking islands of the Caribbean, like la República Dominica and Cuba, is increasing. The larger Mediterranean islands of Mallorca, Menorca and Ibiza depend heavily on tourism as a source of income, as do the Canary Islands. There are also two Spanish-speaking enclaves on the tip of North Africa: Ceuta and Melilla. If you're holidaying in the south of Spain, you might be able to take a day trip across the Mediterranean for a quick visit.

If you travel around, you'll need somewhere to stay. Apart from hotels (**hoteles**), there are campsites (**campings**), youth hostels (**albergues juveniles**) and – if you've got a big budget! – the state-run **paradores**. These luxury hotels are often in historic and beautiful buildings.

Although tourism brings a lot of money to Spain, the unsightly effects (high-rise blocks of flats and hotels) are heavily criticised. Spain has some of the most important wetlands in Europe in the Coto Doñana in the south, and there are a number of **parques naturales**. The recycling of glass (**vidrio**) and paper (**papel**) is widespread, and many young people get involved with environmental groups. So let's get started – **¡vámonos!**

◎ These phrases will be really useful for your exam, so see if you can try and learn them!

Countries and holidays

¿Adónde vas de vacaciones normalmente?
    Where do you usually go on holiday?

Voy a ... Francia, España, Italia, Grecia.
    I go to ... France, Spain, Italy, Greece.

Me quedo en casa.   I stay at home.

Vamos a quedarnos con parientes en ...
    We are going to stay with relatives in ...

¿Para cuánto tiempo vas?
    How long do you go for?

¿Con quién vas?   Who do you go with?

¿Cómo vas?   How do you get there?

¿Dónde te alojas?   Where do you stay?

¿Has visitado España?
    Have you visited Spain?

Sí, conozco la ciudad/la región de ...
    Yes, I know the town/region of ...

No, no la he visitado todavía.
    No, I haven't visited it yet.

¿Adónde fuiste de vacaciones el año pasado?
    Where did you go on holiday last year?

Fui al norte/sur/este/oeste de ...
    I went to the north/south/east/west of ...

¿Qué hiciste?   What did you do?

Nadé en el mar, tomé el sol, saqué fotos.
    I swam in the sea, sunbathed, took
    photos.

¿Qué tipo de vacaciones prefieres?
    What sort of holidays do you prefer?

Prefiero las vacaciones en la playa.
    I prefer holidays at the beach.

en la montaña, en el campo, en la ciudad
    in the mountains, in the country,
    in town

Tourism – hotel bookings

¿Tiene habitaciones libres?
    Have you got any rooms free?

Lo siento, el hotel está completo.
    I'm sorry, the hotel is full.

Quisera una habitación individual con ducha.
    I'd like a single room with a shower.

¿Tiene una habitación doble con baño?
    Have you got a double room with bath?

una habitación con tres camas, con lavabo
    a room with three beds and a basin

una habitación con baño completo
    a room with bath, shower, toilet, basin

¿La habitación tiene vistas al mar?
    Does the room have a seaview?

¿Dónde puedo aparcar el coche?
    Where can I park the car?

¿El desayuno está incluido?
    Is breakfast included?

¿A qué hora se sirve la comida/la cena?
    When is lunch/dinner served?

Mi llave es el número doscientos doce.
    My key is number 212.

The environment

Se debe reciclar papel y vidrio.
    You should recycle paper and glass.

No deberíamos gastar agua/energía.
    We shouldn't waste water/energy.

Es mejor utilizar gasolina sin plomo.
    It's better to use lead-free petrol.

Lo que más me preocupa es ...
    What I'm most worried about is ...

el agujero en la capa de ozono
    the hole in the ozone layer

la guerra, la pobreza, la contaminación
    war, poverty, pollution

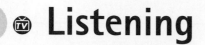
Countries

How many countries of the world do you know in Spanish? Many of them are very similar to the English and you won't have any trouble with places like **Italia** or **India**. But not all countries are as easy as that. Do you know what **Alemania, Suiza, Escocia** and **Gales** are called in English?

Countries are sometimes represented by the initials which are used on car stickers, such as GB for **Gran Bretaña**. Have a go at this activity to brush up on your countries.

! REMEMBER Check with your teacher which symbols your exam board is using to represent countries and learn them.

◎ **Empareja los países con los símbolos.** Match the countries to the symbols.

1 Alemania
2 Austria
3 Escocia
4 España
5 Estados Unidos
6 Francia
7 Grecia
8 Irlanda
9 Italia
10 Israel
11 Portugal
12 Suiza

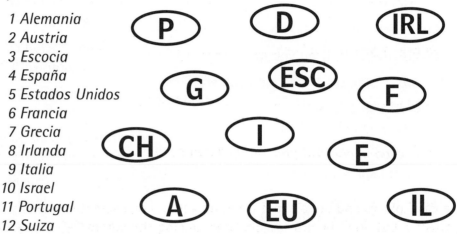

Find the clip where eight people are asked which countries they know: **¿Qué países conoces?** and do the following activity.

◎ **Escucha y rellena la tabla.** Listen and fill in the table.

! REMEMBER Make sure that you know the difference between the name of a country and its language. Don't mix up **España** (Spain) with **el español** (Spanish).

	IRL	I	ING	F	ESC	P	G	EU	D
1									
2									
3									
4									
5									
6									
7									
8									

Tourism

Tourism is a very important industry in Spain, and not just along the coastal regions. Antonio was born in Salamanca, a famous and very beautiful city in the north of Spain. Find the clip in which he introduces himself and do the activity below.

◎ **Escucha y rellena los huecos.** Listen and fill in the gaps.

1 Antonio tiene .... años.

2 El .... de Salamanca se llama el Tormes.

3 El puente es romano y muy ....

4 Hay también muchas ....

5 La .... es muy famosa.

6 El edificio más antiguo de la ciudad es la ....

Names of places and people in a listening activity can sometimes seem confusing, but don't be put off. Try pronouncing the names 1-6 below so that you know what to listen for. Find the clip on Granada which begins : **Granada es una capital andaluza** ... and do the activity below.

◎ **Escucha y empareja los lugares/las personas 1-6 con las explicaciones a-f.** Listen and match up the people/places 1-6 with the explanations a-f.

1 Granada	a un palacio
2 la Alhambra	b reyes católicos
3 Yusuf Primero	c unas islas
4 Cristobal Colón	d una ciudad
5 Fernando e Isabel	e un explorador
6 las Indias	f un rey árabe

REMEMBER If you're not sure of an answer on the first hearing and you write it in rough in the margin, make sure you copy it into the correct space the second time around – the examiner can't give you a mark if there's a blank.

REMEMBER As you do the BITESIZE activities, gradually reduce the time you give yourself to read the question before playing the clip. You'll only have a moment or so between sections of tape in the exam.

You may come across several types of true/false activity in the exam. In the following one, you are asked to tick the true sentences only – always use the example. The example is not included in the number of sentences you have to tick. Find the clip which starts with: **Granada es una capital andaluza** ... and do the activity below.

◎ **Escucha y escribe ✓ al lado de las tres frases verdaderas.**
Listen and write a ✓ beside the three true sentences.

80

! R E M E M B E R
There are several instructions to indicate 'true' and 'false'. You might come across **las frases que son verdad** (true) **o mentira** (false), or **las frases verdaderas** (true) **o falsas** (false).

Ejemplo	La capital es andaluza.	✓
1	Los romanos y los árabes quedaron poco tiempo.	
2	La ciudad tiene influencia árabe.	
3	Los castillos fueron construídos por los romanos.	
4	Isabel y Fernarndo eran reyes cristianos.	
5	Expulsaron a los árabes de España.	

Phrases like **he visitado (Francia)** - I've visited (France) are in the PERFECT tense. This tense is useful in many topic areas when you want to say things such as 'I've lost (my key)', 'I've left (my bag) on the bus' and 'I've fallen on the stairs'. Have a look at how to form this tense below. You will see that you need two parts.

	PERFECT TENSE		IRREGULARS
-ar *(dejar)*	(yo) he	dej**ado** *(I've left)*	escrito *(written)*
-er *(comer)*	(yo) he	com**ido** *(I've eaten)*	hecho *(done)* muerto *(died)* puesto *(put on)*
-ir *(perdir)*	(yo) he	perd**ido** *(I've lost)*	roto *(broken)* visto *(seen)*

◎ What are these people telling you?

1 *He perdido mi reloj, pero no sé dónde.*
2 *¡Ay no! ¡He roto el vaso!*
3 *Hoy, he escrito postales a todos mis amigos.*
4 *He visto esa película en casa.*
5 *¿La mochila? No sé dónde la he dejado.*
6 *¡Claro que he hecho la cama!*

You might want to ask a Spanish teenager: 'Have you visited Great Britain?' Use **has** for 'you have/have you ...?' and **ha** for 'he/she has' and 'has he/she ...?' For example: **Juana <u>ha</u> visitado el país de Gales** means 'Juana has visited Wales'.

◎ Can you work out the correct Spanish to go in the gaps below? The infinitive of the relevant verb is given in brackets at the start of the sentence.

1 *(visitar) .... el sur de Espana?*   Have you visited the south of Spain?
2 *(perder) ¿........................ tu pasaporte? ¡Qué horror!*   You've lost your passport? How awful!
3 *(probar) Sí, ... la tortilla española.*   Yes, I've tried Spanish omelette.
4 *(salido) ¿Irene? .... hace poco.*   Irene? She went out a little while ago.
5 *(dejar) Creo que .... su dinero en casa.*   I think he has left his money at home.

There are two verbs for 'to be' in Spanish: **ser** and **estar**. In general, use **ser** for describing things (size, colour, character, what something's like, permanent states), and use **estar** to indicate a place, say where something or someone is and to indicate temporary states.

◎ Underline the correct words in bold below.

*(1 **Estoy/Soy**) aquí en la isla de Menorca con mi familia. El hotel (2 **está/es**) muy bonito, pero (3 **está/es**) enorme. Nuestra habitación (4 **está/es**) en la tercera planta, con vistas preciosas de la bahía. Los camareros y camareras (5 **están/son**) muy simpáticos, y hay mucha gente joven. El pueblo más cercano (6 **está/es**) a dos kilómetros. (7 **Está/Es**) pequeño pero muy típico de aquí: las casas (8 **están/son**) muy blancas, con balcones llenas de flores. (9 **Estoy/Soy**) muy contento - ¡de momento!*

Speaking

Booking in

Do you remember how to ask for different types of rooms? Look back at the InfoZONE on page 77 if you've forgotten.

(?) Can you explain what you want in each of the situations below?

1	2	3
• single room • two nights • shower	• double bed • seven nights • full bathroom	• three beds • tonight only • wash basin

You might want to stay at a campsite, in which case you'll want to know if there's any room, and you'll need to explain other details as well: how many people, how long for and whether you have a tent (**una tienda**) or a caravan (**una caravana**).

Your exam board might have symbols for role-plays, or it might use prompts in English. Read the example below and work out what you would say. Don't translate the whole sentence into Spanish. Imagine the prompts as a voice whispering in your ear, and work out what message you actually need to convey. For example, in the first line, you simply need: **¿Hay sitio para una tienda?** (Is there room for a tent?) Now you try the rest.

THE EXAMINER	YOU
Buenas tardes. ¿Qué desea?	1 Ask if there's room for a tent.
¿Qué tipo de tienda?	2 Say you've got a large tent and a small one.
¿Para cuántas personas?	3 Say it's for three adults and two children.
¿Para cuántas noches?	4 Tell him it's for three nights.
¿Me da su documento de identidad?	5 Explain that you have a passport.

(h) More complex things might be asked of you at Higher level. The phrase **¿Se puede ...?** (Can you ...?) followed by an infinitive is very useful to know. Supposing you want to know if you can change money on the campsite – simply ask: **¿Se puede cambiar dinero aquí en el camping?** Words like **¿dónde?** (where?) and **¿cuándo?** (when?) can also be used in front of it. How would you say the following?

1 When can you buy bread?

2 Where can you wash clothes?

3 Can you phone from the office?

4 When can you play tennis?

5 Can you swim in the pool at night?

6 Where can you get (**obtener**) ice?

> **! REMEMBER** You won't have much time to use a dictionary when you're preparing for the speaking exam! Learn basic vocabulary – use the InfoZONE pages in this book to help, as well as your own notes.

> **! REMEMBER** You don't need to consult your dictionary for the words for 'Ask if', or 'Explain that'!

Enquiring about facilities

You might have to book into a hotel and ask about facilities. The next activity prepares you to ask some relevant questions.

◎ **Rellena los huecos.** Fill in the gaps.
Ejemplo: 1 ¿El Hotel Malibú?

¿El ...**1**... Malibú?
¿Hay una ...**2**... cubierta?
¿La ...**3**... está lejos?
¿Puedo reservar una ...**4**...
individual?
¿La habitación tiene ...**5**...?
¿Hay ...**6**... en la habitación?
Para cuatro noches, desde las
...**7**... hasta las dieciséis de
septiembre.
¿Se admiten ...**8**... ?

83

The queries above are not in a logical order – but the receptionist's replies below are! See if you can complete the dialogue by adding the queries 1–8. The first two are done for you.

◎ **Completa el diálogo con las frases 1–8.** Complete the dialogue with the sentences 1–8.

1 ¿El Hotel Malibú?
   Sí. ¿En qué puedo servirle?
4 ¿Puedo reservar una habitación individual?
   ¿Cuándo, y para cuánto tiempo?
☐ ....
   Muy bien.
☐ ....
   Sí, se admiten. No hay problema.
☐ ....
   Sí, hay teléfono en todas las habitaciones.
☐ ....
   No, pero hay una en la sala de televisión abajo.
☐ ....
   Sí, y está climatizada.
☐ ....
   No, a unos cien metros.

◎ Now see if you can invent another dialogue with these details.

- a room with two single beds
- a week from the 7–14 August
- shower in the room? (yes)
- seaview? (no, but there's a balcony with a view of the gardens)
- distance to town centre (10 minutes)

Speaking

ⓗ Lost property

REMEMBER Work out the kind of information you need to give and mentally rehearse it. Only if you have forgotten a key word should you look it up in the dictionary. Every moment spent checking the dictionary is one minute less preparation time!

REMEMBER Check with your teacher whether your exam board allows you to take any notes you make during the preparation time into the oral test itself.

REMEMBER If you find it hard to think of the necessary vocabulary, try and imagine yourself back in class when you did or revised the topic – useful words might suddenly come to mind!

In the Higher speaking exam, there might be a more complex task to do which has elements of unpredictability – you might be given some details of a situation in which it is not clear exactly what your teacher or examiner will ask, or in what order. You might be wondering how you can prepare for this – but there are things you can do.

First of all, read the instruction carefully. Where are you, and what has happened or is going to happen? What role does your teacher or examiner play? Are there any pictures or prompts to help?

◎ Read through the activity below, and make a list in English of the kind of things you'll have to say.

Apellidos: ....
Nombre: ....
Domicilio: ....
Nacionalidad: ....
Artículo: ....
Valor: ....
Contenido: ....

> You're on holiday in Spain and you've lost your rucksack. You go to the lost-property office. Your teacher will play the part of the official whose job it is to fill out a report form. Use the information below to guide you as to what to say.
> *Explica a la guardia ...*
> • *qué has perdido y cuándo*
> • *dónde*
> • *cómo era – color, material*
> • *el valor*
> • *qué contenía.*

Your list should contain things like: say I've lost a rucksack, when and where I lost it, give details of the colour and what it's made of, how much it's worth and what was in it. If you are not given specific details, you can make up your own, so choose things you know how to say. Aim high – if you can say more complex things like 'navy blue and bright red' (**azul marino, rojo vivo**) or 'striped' (**de rayas**), add them, so you gain marks for quality of language.

Next, turn your attention to the verbs: what tenses do you need? In this one, you'll need the perfect tense for 'I've lost' (**he perdido**), a preterite tense for 'I lost the rucksack in ...' (**perdí la mochila en ...**), the imperfect tense for 'it contained' (**contenía**) and the present for 'it's ...' (**es ...**).

◎ **Contesta a las preguntas.** Answer the questions.

¿Cómo se llama usted? ¿Qué ha perdido? ¿Cuándo la perdió? ¿Dónde la perdió? ¿Cómo es? ¿Qué contenía? ¿Qué valor tiene?

⑦ You have to expect the unexpected! Your teacher or examiner will almost certainly throw in some extra questions, so think about how you would reply to the following:

1 Habla bien español. ¿Lo aprende desde hace cuánto tiempo?
2 ¿Cuánto tiempo va a quedarse en España?
3 ¿Le gusta España? ¿Por qué (no)?

BITESIZEspanish

Talking about holidays

(📺) Holidays are a popular topic for the speaking exam and you might choose to do your presentation on them. It's a good topic for incorporating a range of tenses and opinions to earn high marks.

As you will see from these four questions, the basic format of opening questions and replies on this topic is very similar and can use three tenses:

	PRESENT	*PRETERITE*	*SIMPLE FUTURE*	
1 ¿Adónde	*vas*	*fuiste*	*vas a ir*	de vacaciones?
	Voy	*fui*	*voy a ir*	(a España).
2 ¿Cuándo	*vas*	*fuiste*	*vas a ir?*	
	Voy	*fui*	*voy a ir*	(en agosto).
3 ¿Cómo	*vas*	*fuiste*	*vas a ir?*	
	Voy	*fui*	*voy a ir*	(en avión).
4 ¿Dónde	*te alojas*	*te alojaste*	*vas a alojarte?*	
	Me alojo	*me alojé*	*voy a alojarme*	(en un hotel).

85

REMEMBER
Listen for 'time phrases': **normalmente/ en general** indicates you need the present tense, **el año/verano pasado** is a hint to use the preterite tense, and **el año que viene/próximo** needs a future tense.

This next question asks what you would do if you had more money (conditional tense).

> *5 Si tuvieras más dinero, ¿adónde te gustaría ir?*
> *Iría (a América del Sur).*

The final question wants to know if you have visited Spain (perfect tense).

> *6 ¿Has visitado España?*
> *Sí, he visitado (la isla de Menorca).*
> *No, no la he visitado todavía.*

REMEMBER
If you make a mistake, just say: ¡Perdón, no es correcto! Quiero decir ...

(❓) See how many questions and answers you can make up using the ones above. For example, if asked: **¿Adónde vas de vacaciones normalmente?** you can reply: **En general, voy a Gales o a Irlanda.**

Practice activity

You might also be asked about what you did on holiday. Look back at the GrammarZONES on pages 49 and 71 to remind yourself of how to form the **yo** (I) part of present, preterite and future verbs.

See how many answers you can give to these three questions.

1 ¿Qué haces normalmente en las vacaciones?
2 ¿Qué hiciste durante tus vacaciones del año pasado?
3 ¿Qué vas a hacer este verano?

EN LA CIUDAD
comprar recuerdos
mirar escaparates
ver una corrida de toros
escribir postales
ir al cine
visitar monumentos
explorar el barrio antiguo
ir al zoo
sacar fotos

EN LA PLAYA/EL CAMPO/LA MONTAÑA
alquilar una bici
descansar
hacer piragüismo
hacer vela
ir de paseo
jugar (al fútbol)
merendar
nadar en el mar/la piscina

The Interntaiona World

Reading

On holiday

This section concentrates on helping you improve your dictionary skills in the reading exam. First, let's focus on looking up nouns. If a noun is singular, it's straightforward to find, but if it's plural, it's unlikely to appear in that form in the dictionary – you need to look it up without the final **'s'** or **'es'**.

◎ Can you find the English meaning of the words underlined in the following extract?

> No me gusta mucho la ciudad: no hay muchos <u>lugares</u> verdes, ni <u>calles</u> peatonales en el centro. En los <u>alrededores</u> hay <u>chabolas</u> sucias en medio de las <u>redes</u> de circunvalaciones – y hay muy pocas <u>instalaciones</u> públicas para la gente que vive allí.

Now, let's focus on adjectives. As they agree with the noun they describe in number (singular or plural) and gender (masculine or feminine) they have a variety of endings. Although there are always exceptions, the following is a useful general guide:

TEXT	DICTIONARY
adjective ending in 'o'	look it up with the ending 'o'
adjective ending in 'a', 'as', 'os'	look it up with the ending 'o'
adjective ending in 'es'	try it without the 'es' ending first; then without the 's'

Read the texts below, in which three Spanish teenagers talk about their impressions of a holiday exchange to Great Britain. The activity focuses on the need to understand the meaning of the adjectives (underlined) so you'll need to do some detective work with your dictionary.

◎ **¿Son las frases verdad o mentira?** Are the sentences true or false?

ELENA
1 A los niños, les gusta mucho la comida.
2 Los niños son un poco antipáticos.

PACO
3 Hay mucho que hacer en la ciudad.
4 Hay muchos estudiantes en el instituto.

CLARA
5 Había mucha gente en las calles.
6 La ciudad era bastante fea.

Los tres niños (6, 8 y 9 años de edad) son muy <u>amables</u>. ¡Pero también son <u>glotones</u>! estan en la cocina todo el tiempo, buscando algo de comer. **(ELENA)**

De noche, el centro de la ciudad está <u>muerta</u> – no sé adónde van todos los jóvenes. Y las aulas del colegio están muy <u>masificadas</u>. **(PACO)**

Fui con la familia a Edimburgo. La ciudad me pareció muy <u>hermosa</u> y de noche las calles y cafeterías estaban <u>llenas</u> y muy <u>animadas</u>. **(CLARA)**

Verbs can be one of the trickier things to look up in a dictionary, especially if they're not in their infinitive form (ending in **-ar, -er, -ir**). This is where recognising the endings which indicate different persons and tenses is important. The extract from Bernardo's letter below is in the present tense and it gives you practice in recognising how different verb endings show which person is doing an activity. Look back at the GrammarZONES on pages 43 and 49 before you start. Bernardo describes what his family does at their holiday home.

◎ **Para cada dibujo, escribe la letra más apropiada (a–e).** For each picture, write the most appropriate letter (a–e).

a *Alicia*
b *Bernardo*
c *Alicia y Bernardo*
d *los padres*
e *toda la familia*

> Mi hermana Alicia es mayor que yo, pero nos llevamos bien y hacemos muchas actividades juntos. Por la tarde, sacamos el perro y damos un paseo por la playa. Charlamos mucho. Si hace mal tiempo, jugamos al ping-pong juntos, pero a veces ella va a la cafetería o da una vuelta en bici con algunos amigos del pueblo. Una vez por semana, Mamá y Papá van de excursión en autocar y de vez en cuando salimos todos en coche para merendar en el campo o visitar iglesias y monumentos históricos. Somos bastantes aficionados a los deportes acuáticos - ¡algunos más que otros! A mis padres les gusta hacer piragüismo cuando vamos a un río en la sierra (yo prefiero echar una siesta) y hacen natación todos los días en la bahía, aún cuando llueve. Me encanta la vela, ¡pero sólo cuando hace calor y sol! (**Bernardo**)

❗ REMEMBER
Make an effort to get to grips with grammar: understanding language patterns can help you when using a dictionary.

❗ REMEMBER
If the ending of the verb is '**a**', '**amos**' or '**an**', try looking it up in the dictionary with an '**ar**' ending. If it ends in '**e**', or '**en**', it might be either an '**er**' or '**ir**' verb. Try both.

Practice activity

h At Higher level, you'll need to identify attitudes and opinions, and justify your answers. Re-read Bernardo's letter and answer the questions below.

1 How would you describe the relationship between Bernardo and his sister? Give a reason for your answer. (2)

2 What can we deduce about Bernardo's attitude to sporting activities? Justify your reply. (2)

3 How would you describe his parent's attitude to sport and keeping fit? Note two facts to support your answer. (3)

Writing

Postcards

Writing postcards is a popular exam activity, and one you can prepare for thoroughly in advance. You might be asked to write about where you're staying, how long you're there for, who you're on holiday with, what you think of the hotel or apartment, what the weather is like and how you spend your time.

REMEMBER
If you're given a model postcard, use it wisely – it might help you to remember little phrases like 'I am', 'it is', and 'the weather is'.

◎ Which one of the above items is not included in this postcard? What does Teresa like? Check your answers at the back!

¡Hola! ¿Qué tal? Estoy aquí de vacaciones en Marbella con mi familia. El hotel es bonito y muy grande, y está cerca de la playa. Me gusta la comida - es muy buena. ¡Hace mucho sol y calor! Juego al fútbol en la playa y nado en la piscina.

Un abrazo,
Teresa.

◎ **Lee la postal. Para cada frase 1–6, busca la frase correspondiente en español.** Read the postcard. For each phrase 1–6, find the Spanish equivalent.

1 I'm here on holiday
2 with my family
3 the hotel is nice
4 it's near the beach
5 the food is good
6 it's very sunny

REMEMBER
Make sure you include all the pieces of information you're asked to give.

(?) Raúl is feeling very negative! Can you write his postcard? He's in Santander with his mum and brother, the hotel is small and old, and it's a long way from the beach. He doesn't like the food (which is awful), and the weather's cold and windy!

Now have a go at this exam-type activity below.

> **Estás de vacaciones en España con tu familia. Escribe una postal a tu amigo/a español/a. Menciona:**
> • dónde estás (Barcelona, Málaga etc.)
> • el hotel/apartamento
> • el tiempo
> • lo que haces durante las vacaciones.

A letter to a campsite

Writing formal letters to hotels or campsites isn't very difficult once you know the format.

◎ Read through this letter and underline the phrases which you think might be useful if you had to write a letter (i.e. 'Dear Sir', 'I'd like to reserve a plot for ...'). Don't underline details like numbers, dates and ages because these are specific to this letter.

> Muy señor mío:
>
> Quisiera visitar el sur de España durante el mes de mayo. Le ruego me reserve espacio en el camping para cinco noches entre el dos y el siete de mayo. Somos cinco personas en total: dos adultos, un joven de dieciséis años, y dos niños de ocho años y diez años. Tenemos un coche y dos tiendas: una tienda familiar y dos tiendas pequeñas.
>
> Quisiera saber también si el camping tiene un supermercado, y a qué distancia del pueblo está. ¿Se puede alquilar bicicletas?
>
> Agradeciéndole su pronto atención,
>
> Le saluda atentamente,
>
> Francisco Aguilar Montero.

REMEMBER Language from one topic area can be used in another: which phrases from this letter could you use when writing to a hotel?

When you're adapting a letter, remember that you might need to make some items plural which were singular in the original letter. For example, the letter above says 'one family tent' but you might need to say you've got two. Genders (masculine and feminine) might also be different – the letter above mentions **un supermercado** but you might have to write about a swimming pool. Can you remember what gender it is?

REMEMBER If you are copying words from a prompt in the exam, make sure you copy correctly - there's no excuse!

Now try writing a letter of your own, using the notes below to help you with the details.

◎ **Escribe una carta con la siguiente información.** Write a letter with the following information.

• north of Spain	• 2 cars
• 7 nights	• 2 family tents
• 22–29 July	• 2 small tents
• 3 adults	• Is there a pool?
• 3 children (6, 9, 11)	• How far to beach?
	• Hire boats?

Writing

The environment

One of the topics you might need to write (or talk) about is the environment. This section will help you put together some ideas. You might want to say what one should do (**se debe ...**), what we should do (**deberíamos ...**) and what would be better or more ecologically helpful (**sería mejor/más ecológico ...**).

◎ Use the grid below to make a list of seven things that you think would help the environment. Use something from each of the columns A, B and C. For example: **No se debe utilizar bolsas de plástico. Deberíamos utilizar menos gasolina.**

A	B	C
(no) se debe *(no) deberíamos* *sería mejor* *sería más ecológico*	*ahorrar* *comprar* *consumir* *evitar* *gastar* *reciclar* *tirar* *utilizar*	*agua* *bolsas de plástico* *bombillas 'eficientes'* *botellas de vidrio* *(más/menos/tanta) energía/gasolina* *productos con muchos envoltorios* *productos enlatados* *ropa usada*

You will have seen from the television programme how you can use **suelo ...** with an infinitive to mean 'I usually ...' in the context of holidays. It can also be used in other topic areas. For example: **Suelo reciclar botellas de vidrio** (I usually recycle glass bottles). You can also use the present tense to express what you do (or don't) do, adding phrases like **normalmente, en general** and **cuando puedo** (when I can). Do you remember how to form the present tense from the infinitive? (Look back at the GrammarZONE on page 49 if you've forgotten.)

Now try and write a paragraph like the one below, saying what you do – or don't do – to help the environment. Use a mixture of the ordinary present tense and **suelo ...** The grid above will help you.

◎ **Escribe un párrafo sobre el medio ambiente.** What do you do to help the environment? Write a paragraph. Start with: **Para ayudar a mejorar el medio ambiente ...**

> *Para ayudar a mejorar el medio ambiente, suelo reciclar papel, ropa usada y botellas de vidrio. No utilizo bolsas de plástico y no compro productos con muchos envoltorios. No gasto mucho agua – suelo tomar una ducha, en vez de bañarme.*

❗ REMEMBER Things you learn to do in writing can also be used in the speaking part of the exam – and vice versa.

❗ REMEMBER As well as the **yo** (I) part of the verb, try to use other parts for variety. You could use the **nosotros** (we) part: **En mi familia, ahorramos energía** (in my family, we save energy).

ⓗ A longer letter or account

At Higher level, you'll be expected to write a longer letter or account of some kind, perhaps for a school magazine. It will be marked under several headings, which usually include 'content' (whether you've included all the information you're asked for), 'quality of language' (your use of vocabulary), and 'accuracy' (tenses, verb·endings etc.).

CONTENT

◎ Look at the Practice activity below and jot down in English what topics you're asked to include. Decide how you might group them into paragraphs (e.g. the first four, then the next two) and which might need a whole paragraph (e.g. the last one). The paragraphs don't need to be all the same length, but they should contain related information.

QUALITY OF LANGUAGE Use as rich a vocabulary as you can. Before the exam, make a list of adjectives which you can use to describe different things (e.g. accommodation, a town and a restaurant) and learn them. In the exam, add adjectives to nouns: **Me alojé en un apartamento moderno y bonito.** Use adverbs, such as **de repente** (suddenly) and **rápidamente** (quickly) and include a range of tenses, such as the preterite to say what you did, the imperfect to describe what things or places were like (**la comida era buenísima**) and the conditional or future to talk about a future holiday.

ACCURACY Check each sentence as you write it, then re-read the whole text over again thoroughly at the end. Look at the following:

NOUNS: are they the correct gender (m/f) and number (singular/plural)?
ADJECTIVES: do they match their noun in number and gender?
VERBS: are they the correct tense? Is the ending correct?
JOINING WORDS: can you join sentences with words like **que** *(which/who) or* **pero** *(but)?*
ADVERBS: can you add words like 'quickly', 'suddenly', 'hurriedly'?

Now have a go at the activity below.

! REMEMBER Ask your teacher for details of how your exam board marks the writing paper: what are the criteria (content, quality of language, accuracy etc.) and what do you have to do to gain as many marks as possible?

! **REMEMBER** Make friends with your dictionary and get to know it well. It might have a useful verb table which can help you check for accuracy.

Practice activity

Pasaste las vacaciones en Tarragona, en España. Escribe un artículo para la revista del colegio describiendo tus experiencias. Menciona:
• con quién fuiste
• cómo fuiste
• cuánto tiempo te quedaste
• dónde te alojaste
• lo que visitaste
• lo que hiciste
• algún excursión que hiciste
• un incidente o accidente que te pasó
• tu opinión de tu estancia en España.

T A R R A G O N A

☞ **GEOGRAFÍA: en la Costa Dorada, noreste de España**

☞ **AEROPUERTO: Reus (20 km)**

☞ **CARÁCTER: antigua ciudad romana**

☞ **MONUMENTOS: anfiteatro, murallas romanas, museos de arqueología/historia**

☞ **PARA VER: barrio medieval, puerto pesquero, playa bonita**

☞ **EXCURSIONES: castillo La Suda (Tortosa), Parc Naturel de Delta de l'Ebre, Monasterio de Poblet (siglo XII)**

Answers

Everyday Activities

📺 Listening

Page 10

School subjects: *1 (history) ✓, 3 (Spanish/language) ✓✓, 4 (English) ✓, 6 (maths) ✓✓✓, 7 (biology) ✓; no-one mentioned 2 geography, 5 computer studies, 8 sport*

Questions: *1 biology, 2 English*

Page 11

True/false activity: *1 mentira, 2 verdad, 3 verdad, 4 mentira, 5 verdad, 6 verdad, 7 mentira, 8 verdad,*

Sentences: *1 room or place, 2 part of body, 3 person, 4 time, 5 room or place*

Susana and Noyer: *1 cuarto de baño, 2 los dientes, 3 mis amigos, 4 ocho y media, 5 el comedor*

Page 12

Underlining: *1 grande, 2 antigua, 3 7, 4 muy, 5 eléctrica*

Yimer's furniture: *1 a/e, 2 d/b, 3 c/f*

Page 13

Places to eat: *Ticks beside: gazpacho, ensalada, filete de cerdo, pescado frito, flan, fruta*

Speaking

Page 14

Question words: *1d, 2c, 3i, 4e, 5c, 6h, 7a, 8j, 9g, 10f*

Fill in the gaps: *1 Dónde, 2 A qué hora, 3 Cuándo, 4 Cuál, 5 Cuánto, 6 Cómo*

Page 15

Times: *las siete de la mañana, las ocho y media de la mañana, las once de la mañana, la una y media de la tarde, las seis de la tarde, las diez y media de la noche*

Mealtimes: *Desayuno a las siete y media. Como/almuerzo a las doce y media. Meriendo a las cuatro y cuarto. Ceno a las seis y media.*

Dialogue: *De primero plato quiero ensalada de tomate. Me gustaría probar la tortilla española y patatas fritas. Para mí, helado de fresa. Quisiera agua mineral con gas.*

Page 16

Parts of the body: *1 la cabeza, 2 la boca, 3 la espalda, 4 la mano, 5 la pierna, 6 la nariz, 7 la garganta, 8 el brazo, 9 el estómago, 10 el pie*

Saying it hurts: *me duelen los ojos, me duele la muñeca, me duelen los oídos, me duele el hombro, me duelen los pies, me duele la muela*

GrammarZONE

Page 17

El/lo/los/las: *la regla, los cuadernos, el sacapuntas, el bolígrafo, la goma, la mochila, el compás, las carpetas*

Gusta/gustan: *1, 3, 5: gusta; 2, 4, 6: gustan*

Matching sentences: *1e, 2a, 3d, 4b, 5c*

Reading

Page 18

School notice: *1 Wednesday, 2 ground floor, 3b, 4c*

Announcements: *1f, 2e, 3c, 4a, 5g, 6d*

Page 19

Menu: *2, 3, 6*

Ben's form: *1 Ben, 2 los huevos, 3 el coliflor, 4 el zumo de fruta, 5 sí*

Page 20

Matching activity: *1c, 2b, 3d, 4f, 5a, 6e*

Nuria's day: *2, 4, 5, 6*

Page 21

Topics: *school and chores are not mentioned*

Who says what?: *1 Alicia, 2 Paco, 3 Alicia, 4 Joaquín, 5 Joaquín, 6 Paco*

Practice activity: *1 18.00, 2 17.30, 3 20.00, 4 22.30, 5 17.00*

Writing

Page 22

Furniture puzzle: *1 cama, 2 guardarropa, 3 alfombra, 4 estante, 5 puerta , 6 mesilla, 7 cómoda, 8 armario*

Page 23

Adjectives: *1 una casa antigua, 2 una entrada pequeña, 3 una nueva cocina, 4 un salón-comedor grande, 5 un cuarto de baño espacioso, 6 una terraza bonita*

Matching activity: *1d, 2g, 3f, 4c, 5a, 6b, 7e*

Page 24

Miguel's letter: *1 arreglar, 2 preparar, 3 barrer, 4 hacer, 5 lavar, 6 pasar*

Phrases: *1 el viernes por la noche, 2 todos los días, 3 el fin de semana, 4 dos veces a la semana, 5 el domingo*

Underlining: *hacer la cama, poner la mesa, sacar la basura, planchar, regar las plantas*

Page 25

Opinions: *Positive 1, 3, 5, 6, 10; Negative 2, 4, 7, 8, 9.*

Arantxa: *7 estúpidas, 9 tontos, 3 divertidas, 10 emocionantes, 6 buenos, 5 estupendas*

Personal Life

📺 Listening

Page 28
Complete the sentences: *1 madre, 2 hermano, 3 hermana, 4 padre*

Form: *personas en casa – 7, hermanos – 2, hermanas – 2, animal – perro.*

Page 29
Complete the sentences: *Sarita - quince, Eduar - doce, Carolina - once, diciembre*

Speech bubbles: *1 Sarita, 2 Carolina, 3 Yimer, 4 Carolina, 5 Eduar, 6 Carolina, 7 Yimer/Sarita*

Page 30
Hobbies grid: *1 a/b/c, 2 a/b, 3 b/d, 4 a/e/f, 5 a/b/d*

Complete the sentences (1): *2 escucho música, 4 leo libros*

Complete the sentences (2): *6 hacer, 7 salir, 8 ir*

Page 31
Times: *13.00 one o'clock/la una, 15.30 half-past three/las tres y media, 20.15 a quarter past eight/las ocho y cuarto, 23.50 ten to twelve/las doce menos diez*

On the phone: *1 ¿Está Enma?, 2 ¿Vamos a la discoteca?, 3 ¿A qué hora?, 4 ¿Dónde quedamos?, 5 ¡De acuerdo!*

At the cinema: *1 two tickets, 2 Manuel liked the film a lot, 3 He's tired, 4 He's going to bed, 5 Vanesa suggests they meet tomorrow*

Practice activity: *1 a/d/f, 2b/e*

Speaking

Page 33
Federico and Ana: *Federico – bajo, fuerte, simpático, alegre; Ana – alta, delgada, habladora*

Alejandro: *1 himself, 2 his brother, 3 himself, 4 himself, 5 his brother, 6 himself, 7 his brother*

Page 34
Javi and Marifé: *1 el, 2 de, 3 por, 4 el, 5 por, 6 por*

Matching activity: *1d, 2c, 3b, 4e, 5a*

Meeting up: *1 enfrente del parque/a las cinco y cuarto, 2 delante de la cafetería/a las once, 3 al lado del cine/a las nueve, 4 detrás de la iglesia/a la una menos cuarto*

Page 35
Time phrases: *1 en verano/en otoño/en invierno, 2 en septiembre, 3 una vez por mes, 4 tres veces por semana, 5 los lunes por la noche, 6 martes/sabados, 7 el dieciséis de junio*

Conversation: *1 en invierno, 2 en julio y agosto, 3 dos veces por semana, 4 después de las clases, 5 los viernes por la noche, 6 los domingos*

Reading

Page 36
Club poster: *1 under sixteens, 2 Tuesdays and Thursdays, 3 (two of) canoeing, climbing, swimming, sailing, 4 July and August*

Sports: *1f, 2e, 3b, 4a, 5g, 6d, 7c*

Nuria's letter: *1 verdad, 2 mentira, 3 mentira, 4 verdad, 5 mentira, 6 verdad*

Page 37
Invitations: *A3, B4, C5, D7, E1, F2*

The appropriate person: *1C, 2F, 3A, 4D, 5E, 6B*

Page 38
Underlining (1): *1 aburrido, 2 peligroso, 3 cara, 4 competitivo.*

Underlining (2): *1 hermana, 2 deportes, 3 amigo, 4 chicas.*

Letters in boxes: *7, 6, 3, 8, 4, 9, 5*

Page 39
Pocket money: *Cosas para comer - 3, 5, 9; Ropa - 2, 10, 12; Lugares de diversión - 1, 7, 13; Música - 4, 6, 8; Cosas para leer - 11, 14, 15*

Practice activity: *1 Isabel, 2 Isabel, 3 Enrique, 4 Sabrina, 5 Paul, 6 Paul*

Writing

Page 40
Sports: *a el tenis, b la vela, c el fútbol, d la natación, e el baloncesto, f el esquí, g el ciclismo, h el ping-pong*

Juego/practico: *a juego al tenis, b practico la vela, c juego al fútbol, d practico la natación, e juego al baloncesto, f practico el esquí, g practico el ciclismo, h juego al ping-pong*

Page 41
Sentences: *Felipe - me gusta practicar el footing/hacer footing, pero no me gusta jugar al golf. Catalina - me gusta practicar el alpinismo/hacer alpinismo, pero no me gusta jugar al voleibol. Raúl - me gusta practicar el piragüismo/hacer piragüismo, pero no me gusta jugar al rugby. Javier - me gusta jugar al hockey, pero no me gusta practicar la equitación/hacer equitación.*

GrammarZONE

Page 43
Subject pronouns: *yo - I, tú - you (one person, familiar), él - he, ella - she, usted - you (one person, formal), nosotros - we, vosotros - you (more than one person, familiar), ellos - they (male), ellas - they (female), ustedes - you (more than one person, formal)*

Clara's family: *1 soy, 2 tengo, 3 son, 4 tiene, 5 es, 6 somos, 7 tiene, 8 soy, 9 va, 10 vamos, 11 sois*

The World Around Us

📺 Listening

Page 46
Mexico City: 1 - 19, 2 - 30, 3 - 2000, 4 - ¼, 5 - ½

Town/village: 2, 4, 6, 8

Page 47
Zujaira: 1d, 2i, 3b, 4g, 5a, 6h, 7c, 8e

Maps: *la farmacia b, la panadería c, la zapatería a*

Page 48
Clothes: *Vanesa – azul marino, Israel _ blanca, Ramón – rojo, Sara – gris.*

Multiple-choice: *1a, 2b, 3a, 4b, 5c, 6a*

Practice activity: *a doscientas pesetas, b quinientas noventa y cinco pesetas, c ochocientas cinco pesetas, d mil cuatrocientas treinta y cinco pesetas, e cinco mil setecientas veinte pesetas. f diez mil novecientas noventa y nueve pesetas.*

GrammarZONE

Page 49
Infinitives: *1 explorar, 2 buscar, 3 comprar, 4 gastar, 5 volver*

Clara's letter: *1 vivo, 2 escucho, 3 leo, 4 hago, 5 practica, 6 salimos*

Speaking

Page 50
Answer the questions: *1 Hay una en la Plaza mayor. 2 Hay uno en la Avenida de Cádiz. 3 Hay una en la esquina de la Avenida de Cádiz y el Paseo de San Juan. 4 Hay una en la Calle Goya. 5 Hay una en la esquina de la Plaza Mayor y la Calle Goya.*

Dialogue: *1 por aquí, 2 uno, 3 enfrente, 4 la cafetería, 5 gracias*

Page 51
Directions: *1 baje la calle – go down the street, 2 tuerza a la izquierda – turn left, 3 tome la primera a la izquierda - take the first on the left, 4 siga todo recto – carry straight on, 5 al final de la calle – to/at the end of the street, 6 cruce la plaza – cross the square, 7 tuerza a la derecha – turn right, 8 tome la segunda a la derecha – take the second right, 9 hasta el cruce – as far as the crossroads, 10 hasta los semáforos – as far as the traffic lights*

Page 52
Tickets: *1 un billete sencillo/de ida sólo para Madrid, 2 un billete no-fumador, 3 un billete de primera clase, 4 un billete de ida y vuelta para Calahorra, 5 dos billetes sencillos/de ida sólo para Zaragoza, 6 un carnet de diez viajes, 7 un billete de segunda clase*

First dialogue: *Quisiera un billete de ida y vuelta, no fumador, para Toledo por favor. De segunda clase. ¿A qué hora llega el tren a Toledo? ¿De qué andén sale? Gracias, adiós.*

Page 53
Items: *1a, 2 h/k, 3f, 4 c/d, 5 e/g, 6h, 7i, 8 c/d, 9g, 10b, 11j*

Reading

Page 54
Poster: *2, 3, 4, 6*

Signs: *A5, B1, C9, D7, E2, F8, G4, H3*

Page 55
Ecuador: *Costa (estación seca) e, i, d; Sierra (estación de las lluvias) h, b, g*

Weather forecast: *1 Cataluña, 2 Cantábrico, 3 Castilla y León, 4 Islas Baleares, 5 Andalucía*

Page 56
Multiple-choice: *1b, 2c, 3a, 4c, 5b, 6b*

Page 57
Mercedes: *1g, 2a, 3f, 4h, 5d, 6b, 7e, 8c*

Practice activity: *1c, 2a, 3b, 4e, 5g, 6d*

Writing

Page 59
Gap-filling: *1 la costa, 2 río, 3 el campo, 4 las montañas/la sierra, 5 el centro, 6 norte, 7 noreste, 8 este, 9 sureste*

Adjectives: *El pueblo es: bonito, acogedor, antiguo, turístico, tranquilo, histórico. La ciudad es: fea, aburrida, ruidosa, pequeña, animada, moderna*

The World of Work

📺 Listening

Page 62
Types of words: *1 number, 2 verb, 3 school subject, 4 place, 5 adjective*

Gap-filling: *1 dieiocho, 2 tenemos, 3 educación física, 4 universidad, 5 buen*

Maite: *Chica 1 - C/E, Bachir - A, Chica 2 - F/B, Chico 1 - D*

Page 63
Virginia's friends: *1D, 2C, 3E, 4F, 5A*

Isabel/Carmen: *1c, 2a, 3b, 4c, 5a, 6b*

Speaking

Page 64
Phone call: *1 ¿Diga? 2 ¿Está Ana? 3 ¿Puedo dejar un recado? 4 Volveré a llamar más tarde, a eso de las nueve. 5 Soy (John). 6 Gracias y adiós.*

Hotel Santa Fé: *1e, 2h, 3f, 4d, 5a, 6b, 7g, 8c*

Page 65
Gap-filling: *1 sábados, 2 siete, 3 nueve, 4 cuatro, 5 ochocientas, 6 interesante*

Page 66
Matching activity: *1e, 2c, 3g, 4a, 5f, 6d, 7h, 8b*

Reading

Page 68
Curriculum vitae: *1 García Morales, 2 Carmen, 3 17 años, 4 10-4-1982, 5 Lima, Perú, 6 Peruana, 7 Soltera, 8 36 741 802C, 9 Calle San Agustín, 18, 2oD, 28002, Madrid, 10 (91) 746 65 71, 11 Instituto San Ignacio, Madrid (BUP, COU), 12 Prácticas de trabajo en el Hospital Juan de Dios, 13 Fotografía/baloncesto, 14 Médico,*

Page 69
Job adverts: *Begoña 4, David 3, Juanjo 1*

Page 70
Tenses: *1 PS, 2 PS, 3 PT, 4 PT, 5 F, 6 F, 7 F, 8 F*

Practice activity: *1 De lunes a viernes trabajo como dependiente en una frutería. 2 Los sábados y domingos, ayudo a mi tío en su taller – es mecánico. 3 Pasé ocho días laborables allí. 4 mejor todavía era preparar folletos turísticos en el ordenador. 5 quiero seguir estudiando el año próximo y hacer el COU. 6 Me interesa mucho el sector del turismo. 7 Me gusta mucho ayudar a la gente. 8 Tal vez iré a vivir en otro país sudaméricano.*

GrammarZONE

Page 71
Match phrases: *1e, 2f, 3b, 4c, 5a, 6d*

Translate sentences: *1 Hice mi experencia laboral/mis prácticas de trabajo en una oficina. 2 Iba en autobús. 3 Tenía que archivar y hacer el café. 4 Era un poco aburrido y repetitivo. 5 No trabajaré en una oficina en el futuro. 6 Iré al extranjero si es posible.*

Writing

Page 72
Jobs: *1 un estudiante/a student, 2 un cantante/a singer, 3 un fotógrafo/a photographer, 4 un enfermero/a nurse, 5 un profesor/a teacher, 6 un programador/a programmer, 7 un dependiente/a shop assistant, 8 un abogado/a lawyer, 9 un comerciante/a business person, 10 un ingeniero/an engineer, 11 un médico/a doctor*

Page 74
Letter: *1 cuatro, 2 camping, 3 puestos, 4 verano, 5 lengua, 6 asignaturas, 7 bastante, 8 útil, 9 niños, 10 responsable, 11 empezar/comenzar, 12 finales*

Page 75
Future plans: *1 Quiero trabajar en la enseñanza con niños pequeños. 2 Voy a seguir estudiando en el colegio. 3 Quisiera buscar un empleo manual. 4 Me gustaría tener mi propia empresa. 5 Quiero viajar en el extranjero. 6 Quisiera trabajar en un equipo, en los servicios médicos.*

The International World

📺 Listening

Page 78

Countries symbols: *1 D, 2 A, 3 ESC, 4 E, 5 EU, 6 F, 7 G, 8 IRL, 9 I, 10 IL, 11 P, 12 CH*

Countries grid: *1 F, G. 2 G, I, ING. 3 INGF. 4 ING. 5 ING, D. 6 ING, ESC, IRL, F, P. 7 EU, F. 8 EU, ING*

Page 79

Gap-filling: *1 quince, 2 río, 3 antiguo, 4 iglesias. 5 Plaza Mayor. 6 la universidad*

Places/people: *1d, 2a, 3f, 4e, 5b, 6c*

Page 80

Granada: *you should have ticks beside sentences 2, 4, 5*

GrammarZONE

Page 81

What are these people telling you?: *1 I've lost my watch, but I don't know where. 2 Oh, no! I've broken the glass! 3 Today I've written postcards to all my friends. 4 I've seen this film at home. 5 The rucksack? I don't know where I've left it. 6 Of course I've made my bed!*

Gap-filling: *1 ¿Has visitado le sur de España? 2 ¿Has perdido tu pasaporte? ¡Qué horror! 3 Sí, he probado la tortilla española. 4 ¿Irene? Ha salido hace poco. 5 Creo que ha dejado su dinero en casa.*

Ser/estar: *1 estoy, 2 es, 3 es, 4 está, 5 son, 6 está, 7 es, 8 son, 9 estoy.*

Speaking

Page 82

Campsite dialogue: *1 ¿Hay sitio para una tienda? 2 Tengo una tienda grande y una tienda pequeña. 3 Para tres adultos y dos niños. 4 Para tres noches. 5 Tengo un pasaporte.*

Se puede: *1 ¿Cuándo se puede comprar pan? 2 ¿Dónde se puede lavar la ropa? 3 ¿Se puede telefonar desde la oficina? 4 ¿Cuándo se puede jugar al tenis? 5 ¿Se puede nadar en la piscina por la noche? 6 ¿Dónde se puede obtener hielo?*

Page 83

Hotel: *1 hotel, 2 piscina, 3 playa, 4 habitación, 5 teléfono, 6 televisión, 7 doce, 8 perros*

Hotel dialogue: *(in this order) 1, 4, 7, 8, 5, 6, 2, 3*

Reading

Page 86

Nouns: *lugares – places, calles – streets, alrededores – outskirts, chabolas – shanty towns, redes – networks, instalaciones – facilities*

Holiday exchange: *1 verdad, 2 mentira, 3 mentira, 4 verdad, 5 verdad, 6 mentira*

Page 87

Bernardo's letter: *1d, 2a, 3c, 4b, 5d, 6e, 7c, 8e*

Higher level activity: *1 The relationship seems to be a good one. They do a lot of activites together, 2 Bernardo is a bit lazy when it comes to sport. He prefers to have a nap under a tree when his parents go canoeing, and he only likes sailing when it's hot and sunny, 3 His parents are very active. They go canoeing in mountain rivers and they swim every day of the holidays in the sea even when it's raining.*

Writing

Page 88

Postcard: *Item not included is 'how long you're there for'. Teresa likes the food.*

Find the Spanish: *1 Estoy aquí de vacaciones, 2 con mi familia, 3 el hotel es bonito, 4 está cerca de la playa, 5 la comida es buena, 6 hace mucho sol*

Page 89

Letter: *Muy señor mío,*
Quisiera visitar el norte de España durante el mes de julio. Le ruego me reserve espacio en el camping para siete noches entre el veintdós y el veintinueve de julio. Somos seis personas en total: tres adultos, y tres niños de seis años, nueve años y once años. Tenemos dos coches y cuatro tiendas: dos tiendas familiares y dos tiendas pequeñas.
Quisiera saber también si el camping tiene una piscina, y a qué distancia de la playa está. ¿Se puede alquilar barcos?
Agradeciéndole su pronto atención,
Le saluda atentamente ...